free spirit
KNITS

20
KNITTED GARMENTS AND
ACCESSORIES INSPIRED
BY THE SOUTHWEST

ANNE PODLESAK

INTERWEAVE
interweave.com

Contents

Introduction

The high desert area of the southwestern United States encompasses many different types of gorgeous vistas—from mountains to arroyos, mesas to valleys. This area has inspired many different types of artistic creations, including jewelry and pottery from the local Native American artisans, as well as the painted works of Georgia O'Keeffe. These beautiful and majestic landscapes inspired this collection of men's and women's sweaters and accessories for the handknitter.

The deciduous aspen covers many mountain slopes across the Rockies. The trees' vivid golden-yellow leaves are a sure sign of fall in the western mountains. As soon as I can look across the valley to Taos Mountain and see vibrant patches of yellow, I know it's time for the Taos Sheep and Wool Festival, an annual pilgrimage for me every year in early October.

Aspens SWEATER

Finished Size
About 34¼ (36, 38¼, 40½, 44¾, 49, 53)" (87 [91.5, 97, 103, 113.5, 124.5, 134.5] cm) bust circumference, and 20¾ (21½, 22½, 23, 23½, 24, 24¾)" (52.5 [54.5, 57, 58.5, 59.5, 61, 63] cm) long.

Project shown measures 36" (91.5 cm).

Yarn
Fingering weight (Super Fine #1).

Shown here: Brooklyn Tweed Loft (100% American wool; 275 yd/1¾ oz [50 g]): #21 Hayloft, 5 (5, 5, 6, 6, 7, 7) skeins.

Needles
Body: Size U.S. 4 (3.5 mm) 24" (60 cm) or longer circular (cir).

Adjust needle size if necessary to obtain the correct gauge.

Notions
Stitch markers (m); stitch holders or waste yarn; pair of size U.S. 4 (3.5 mm) double-pointed needles (dpn) for three-needle BO; tapestry needle; 7 (7, 7, 7, 9, 9, 9) ⅝" (1.5 cm) buttons.

Gauge
26 sts and 37 rows = 4" (10 cm) in St st, after blocking; each 15-st *Aspen Leaf* panel = 2½" (6.5 cm) wide.

Notes

The chart is worked back and forth. Read all right-side (odd-numbered) rows from right to left and all wrong-side (even-numbered) rows from left to right.

*The lace chart begins with 15 stitches, increases to 17 sts on Row 5, to 19 sts on Row 7, then decreases to 17 sts on Row 9, and to 15 sts on Row 11. Stitch counts should not be taken on chart Rows 5 through 10. To ensure your stitch counts will match those in the pattern, begin the armhole and neck decreases on **Aspen Leaf chart** Row 2, 4, or 11.*

Slip the first stitch of each row of the body to help provide a smooth, even edge to pick up the buttonband sts.

A cir needle is used to accommodate the large number of stitches. Work back and forth.

Design Notebook

This project is a woman's cardigan sweater with waist shaping for a tailored silhouette. The sweater is knitted in one piece from the bottom up to the armholes. The fronts and back are then shaped separately and joined at the shoulders with three-needle bind-off. The cap sleeves are worked flat, seamed, and set into the armholes. A wide panel of leaf lace adorns the back, while a single panel of the same motif highlights the front cardigan opening and the sleeves. A simple garter stitch finishes the hems, the neckband, and the front bands.

Body

With cir needle, CO 221 (233, 247, 261, 287, 313, 339) sts using the long-tail cast-on method (see Techniques). Do not join.

SET-UP ROW: (WS) Sl 1, k1, place marker (pm), k15, pm, k38 (41, 45, 48, 54, 61, 67), pm for left side, k32 (35, 38, 42, 49, 55, 62), pm, k47, pm, k32 (35, 38, 42, 49, 55, 62), pm for right side, k38 (41, 45, 48, 54, 61, 67), pm, k15, pm, k2.

NEXT ROW: Sl 1, k1, *sm, knit to m; rep from * 7 more times, work to end.

Rep last row once more.

NEXT ROW: (RS) Sl 1, k1, sm, work Row 1 of *Aspen Leaf chart* over next 15 sts, sm, (knit to next m, sm) twice, (work Row 1 of *Aspen Leaf chart* over next 15 sts, k1) twice, work Row 1 of *Aspen Leaf chart* over next 15 sts, sm, (knit to m, sm) twice, work Row 1 of *Aspen Leaf chart* over next 15 sts, sm, k2.

NEXT ROW: (WS) Sl 1, p1, sm, work Row 2 of *Aspen Leaf chart* over next 15 sts, sm, (purl to next m, sm) twice, (work Row 2 of *Aspen Leaf chart* over next 15 sts, p1) twice, work Row 2 of *Aspen Leaf chart* over next 15 sts, sm, (purl to m, sm) twice, work Row 2 of *Aspen Leaf chart* over next 15 sts, sm, p2.

Work 12 more rows as established.

SHAPE WAIST

DEC ROW: (RS) *Work to 3 st before side m, ssk, k1, sm, k1, k2tog; rep from * once more, work to end—4 sts dec'd.

Rep Dec row every 12 rows 4 more times—201 (213, 227, 241, 267, 293, 319) sts rem.

Work 11 rows even. Piece should measure 8¼" (21 cm) from beg.

SHAPE BUST

INC ROW: (RS) *Work to 1 st before side m, m1r, k1, sm, k1, m1l; rep from * once more, work to end—4 sts inc'd.

ASPEN LEAF CHART

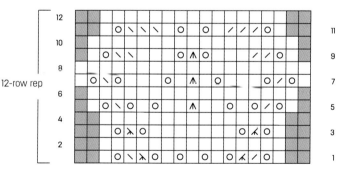

12-row rep

	k on RS; p on WS		ssk		sssk
	yo		sk2p		no stitch
	k2tog		k3tog		

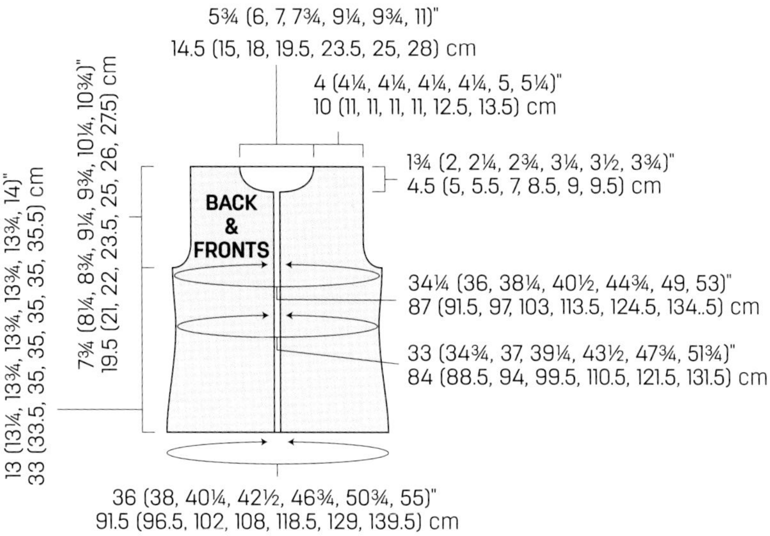

5¾ (6, 7, 7¾, 9¼, 9¾, 11)"
14.5 (15, 18, 19.5, 23.5, 25, 28) cm
4 (4¼, 4¼, 4¼, 4¼, 5, 5¼)"
10 (11, 11, 11, 11, 12.5, 13.5) cm
1¾ (2, 2¼, 2¾, 3¼, 3½, 3¾)"
4.5 (5, 5.5, 7, 8.5, 9, 9.5) cm
BACK & FRONTS
34¼ (36, 38¼, 40½, 44¾, 49, 53)"
87 (91.5, 97, 103, 113.5, 124.5, 134..5) cm
33 (34¾, 37, 39¼, 43½, 47¾, 51¾)"
84 (88.5, 94, 99.5, 110.5, 121.5, 131.5) cm
13 (13¼, 13¾, 13¾, 13¾, 13¾, 14)"
33 (33.5, 35, 35, 35, 35, 35.5) cm
7¾ (8¼, 8¾, 9¼, 9¾, 10¼, 10¾)"
19.5 (21, 22, 23.5, 25, 26, 27.5) cm
36 (38, 40¼, 42½, 46¾, 50¾, 55)"
91.5 (96.5, 102, 108, 118.5, 129, 139.5) cm

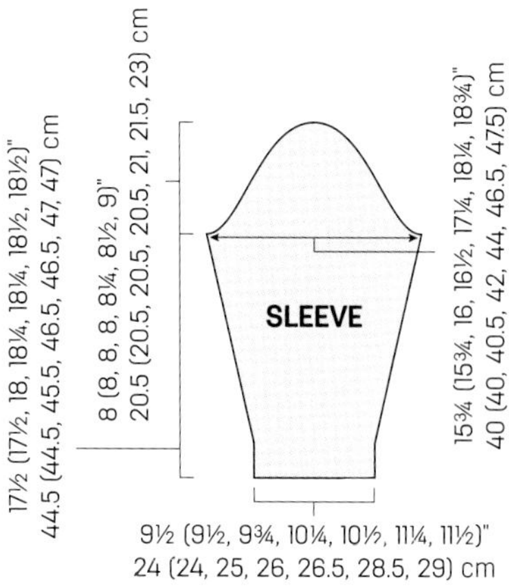

SLEEVE
17½ (17½, 18, 18¼, 18¼, 18½, 18½)"
44.5 (44.5, 45.5, 46.5, 46.5, 47, 47) cm
8 (8, 8, 8¼, 8½, 9)"
20.5 (20.5, 20.5, 21, 21.5, 23) cm
15¾ (15¾, 16, 16½, 17¼, 18¼, 18¾)"
40 (40, 40.5, 42, 44, 46.5, 47.5) cm
9½ (9½, 9¾, 10¼, 10½, 11¼, 11½)"
24 (24, 25, 26, 26.5, 28.5, 29) cm

Rep Inc row every 14 rows once more—209 (221, 235, 249, 275, 301, 327) sts.

Cont even until piece measures 13 (13¼, 13¾, 13¾, 13¾, 13¾, 14)" (33 [33.5, 35, 35, 35, 35, 35.5] cm) from beg, ending with a WS row.

SHAPE ARMHOLES

NEXT ROW: (RS) *Work to 4 (4, 4, 5, 5, 6, 6) sts before side m, BO 8 (8, 8, 10, 10, 12, 12) sts, removing m; rep from * once more, work to end—48 (51, 55, 57, 63, 69, 75) sts rem for each front, and 97 (103, 109, 115, 129, 139, 153) sts rem for back.

LEFT FRONT

Work 1 WS row even.

BO at beg of RS rows 2 (2, 2, 2, 3, 3, 3) sts once, then 1 st 2 (2, 2, 2, 3, 3, 3) times—44 (47, 51, 53, 57, 63, 69) sts rem.

Cont even until armhole measures 6 (6¼, 6½, 6½, 6½, 6¾, 7)" (15 [16, 16.5, 16.5, 16.5, 17, 18] cm), ending with a RS row.

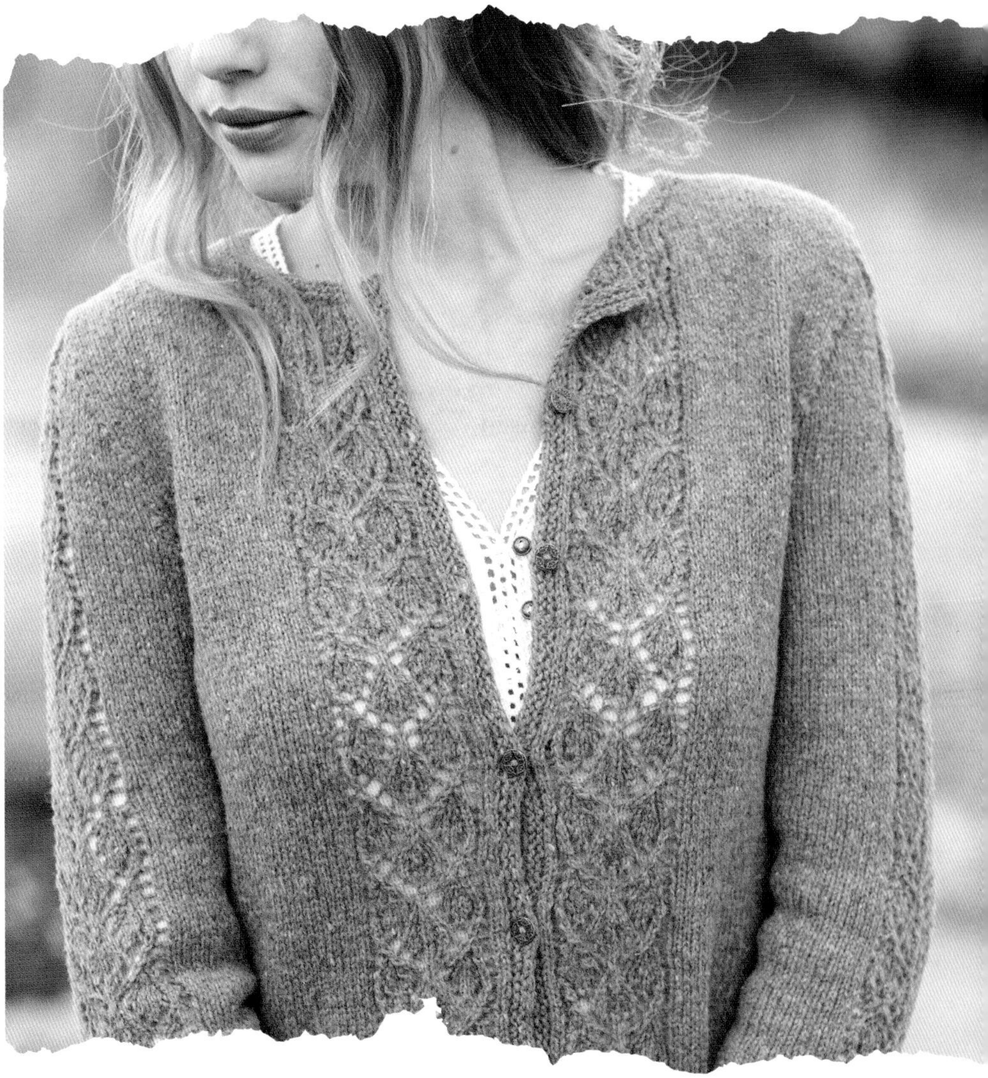

SHAPE NECK

BO at beg of WS rows 12 sts once, 3 (3, 3, 4, 4, 4, 4) sts twice, then 1 (1, 2, 1, 2, 2, 2) st(s) 1 (2, 3, 6, 5, 6, 8) time(s)—25 (27, 27, 27, 27, 31, 33) sts rem.

Work even until armhole measures 7¾ (8¼, 8¾, 9¼, 9¾, 10¼, 10¾)" (19.5 [21, 22, 23.5, 25, 26, 27.5] cm), ending with WS row. Place rem sts on holder.

RIGHT FRONT

Join yarn to beg with a WS row.

BO at beg of WS rows 2 (2, 2, 2, 3, 3, 3) sts once, then 1 st 2 (2, 2, 2, 3, 3, 3) times—44 (47, 51, 53, 57, 63, 69) sts rem.

Cont even until armhole measures 6 (6¼, 6½, 6½, 6½, 6¾, 7)" (15 (16, 16.5, 16.5, 16.5, 17, 18] cm), ending with a WS row.

SHAPE NECK

At beg of RS rows, BO 12 sts once, 3 (3, 3, 4, 4, 4, 4) sts twice, then 1 (1, 2, 1, 2, 2, 2) st(s) 1 (2, 3, 6, 5, 6, 8) time(s)—25 (27, 27, 27, 27, 31, 33) sts rem.

Work even until armhole measures 7¾ (8¼, 8¾, 9¼, 9¾, 10¼, 10¾)" (19.5 [21, 22, 23.5, 25, 26, 27.5]cm), ending with WS row. Place rem sts on holder.

Back

Join yarn to beg with a WS row.

BO 2 (2, 2, 2, 3, 3, 3) sts at beg of next 2 rows—93 (99, 105, 111, 123, 133, 147) sts rem. Dec 1 st at each end of every RS row 2 (2, 2, 2, 3, 3, 3) times—89 (95, 101, 107, 117, 127, 141) sts rem.

Work even until armholes measure 7¾ (8¼, 8¾, 9¼, 9¾, 10¼, 10¾)" (19.5 [21, 22, 23.5, 25, 26, 27.5] cm), ending with a RS row.

NEXT ROW: (WS) Purl, removing m. With RS facing, place first 25 (27, 27, 27, 27, 31, 33) sts on holder for shoulder, center 39 (41, 47, 53, 63, 65, 75) sts on holder for neck, then rem 25 (27, 27, 27, 27, 31, 33) sts on holder for shoulder.

Sleeves

With cir needle, CO 59 (59, 61, 63, 65, 69, 71) sts using long-tail cast-on method. Do not join.

SET-UP ROW: (WS) K22 (22, 23, 24, 25, 27, 28) sts, pm, k15, pm, k22 (22, 23, 24, 25, 27, 28).

NEXT ROW: (RS) *Knit to m, sm; rep from * once more, work to end.

Rep last row once more.

NEXT ROW: (RS) Knit to m, sm, work Row 1 of *Aspen Leaf chart* over next 15 sts, sm, knit to end.

NEXT ROW: (WS) Purl to m, sm, work Row 2 of *Aspen Leaf chart* over next 15 sts, sm, purl to end.

Work 22 (22, 22, 22, 22, 10, 10) more rows in established patt.

INC ROW: (RS) K1, m1l, work in established patt to last st , m1r, k1—2 sts inc'd.

Rep Inc row every 6 rows 9 (9, 9, 10, 10, 10, 13) times, then every 8 rows 9 (9, 9, 9, 10, 11, 9) times—97 (97, 99, 103, 107, 113, 117) sts.

Cont even until piece measures 17½ (17½, 18, 18¼, 18¼, 18½, 18½)" (44.5 [44.5, 45.5, 46.5, 46.5, 47, 47] cm), from beg, ending with a WS row.

SHAPE CAP

BO 4 (4, 4, 5, 5, 6, 6) sts at beg of next 2 rows, then 3 (3, 3, 3, 4, 4, 4) sts at beg of next 2 rows. Dec 1 st at each end of every RS row 32 (32, 32, 33, 34, 35, 37) times—19 (19, 21, 21, 21, 23, 23) sts rem.

BO 2 sts at beg of next 4 rows—11 (11, 13, 13, 13, 15, 15) sts rem.

Work 1 WS row even

BO rem sts kwise.

Finishing

Weave in all the loose ends. Join the shoulders using the three-needle bind-off (see Techniques).

NECKBAND

With cir needle and RS facing, pick up and k21 (22, 24, 27, 28, 30, 30) sts along right front neck, k39 (41, 47, 53, 61, 65, 75) held sts for back neck, then pick up and k21 (22, 24, 27, 28, 30, 30) sts along left front neck—81 (85, 95, 107, 117, 125, 135) sts.

Knit 3 rows. BO all sts loosely kwise.

BUTTONBAND

With cir needle and RS facing, beg at left neck edge, pick up and k3 sts in neckband, 1 st in every sl st along left front edge, then 3 sts in garter st band at bottom.

Knit 3 rows. BO all sts loosely kwise.

PM FOR BUTTONS AS FOLL: Bottom button ½" (1.3 cm) from CO edge, top button ½" (1.3 cm) from BO edge of neckband, then evenly space rem buttons in between.

BUTTONHOLE BAND

With cir needle and RS facing, beg at bottom edge, pick up and k3 sts in garter st band at bottom, 1 st in every sl st along right front edge, then 3 sts in neckband.

NEXT ROW: (WS) *Knit to 1 st before m, k2tog, yo; rep from * 6 (6, 6, 6, 8, 8, 8) more times, knit to end.

Knit 1 row.

BO all sts loosely kwise.

Sew the underarm seams. Sew in the sleeves. Allow the garment to soak in lukewarm water until thoroughly saturated. Gently press or spin out the excess water. Lay garment out to measurements, pinning hems so that they dry flat. Allow the garment to dry completely. Sew buttons to the button-band opposite the buttonholes.

The Grand Canyon is one of the best-known vacation destinations in the Southwest United States. Carved by the fast-moving waters of the Colorado River, the canyon was sliced through layers of striated rock to a mile deep in some locations. Photos of the canyon only hint at the breathtaking beauty with colors that change with the smallest shift in sunlight during the day. While the canyon is gorgeous any time of the year, my favorite time to visit is late winter when there is still snow on the north sides of the rock faces, and you can enjoy a long sunrise, watching the light creep along each rock formation and shimmer off the snow.

Grand Canyon
COAT

Finished Size
About 31 (33, 34¾, 36¾, 38½, 42, 46¼, 50)" (79 [84, 88.5, 93.5, 98, 106.5, 117.5, 127] cm) bust circumference, including ½" (1.3 cm) I-cord edgings, and 35 (35½, 35½, 35½, 36, 36½, 36½, 37)" (89 [90, 90, 90, 91.5, 92.5, 92.5, 94] cm) long.

Project shown measures 33" (84 cm).

Yarn
Worsted weight (#4 Medium).

SHOWN HERE: Dream in Color Classy (100% superwash merino wool; 250 yd/4 oz [113 g]): #320 Chinatown Apple (A), 5 (5, 6, 7, 7, 8, 9, 10) skeins; #611 Blue Sulk (B), 1 (1, 2, 2, 2, 3, 3) skein(s); #42 Atomic Blue (C), 1 (1, 2, 2, 2, 2, 2, 2) skein(s); #10 Gold Experience (D), 1 (1, 2, 2, 2, 2, 2, 2) skein(s).

Needles
MAIN BODY AND SLEEVES AND I-CORD FRONT BANDS: Size U.S. 7 (4.5 mm) 24" (60 cm) or longer circular (cir), and set of 4 or 5 double-pointed (dpn).

BODY AND SLEEVE HEMS, AND WAIST: Size U.S. 8 (5 mm) 24" (60 cm) or longer circular (cir), and set of 4 or 5 double-pointed (dpn).

Adjust needle size if necessary to obtain the correct gauge.

Notions
Stitch markers (m); waste yarn or stitch holders; 2 spare dpn for attached I-cord bands; tapestry needle; 7 (7, 7, 7, 9, 9, 9, 9) 1" (25 mm) buttons, sewing thread; sewing needle.

Gauge
21 sts and 27 rows = 4" (10 cm) in St st using size U.S. 7 (4.5 mm) needles worked flat, after blocking.

21 sts and 25½ rows = 4" (10 cm) in chart patterns using size U.S. 8 (5 mm) needles worked flat, after blocking.

(see Techniques).

Notes
The Hem and Waistband charts are worked back and forth. Read the right-side (odd-numbered) rows from right to left and the wrong-side (even-numbered) rows from left to right. The Sleeve chart is worked in the round; read all the rounds from right to left.

A circular needle is used to work the body back and forth in order to accommodate the number of stitches. Work back and forth, do not join.

Design Notebook

This woman's jacket features a stockinette body with colorwork bands at the hem and waistline and wide colorwork cuffs. The colorwork sections at the hem and waistline are knit back and forth, while the cuffs are knit in the round. The garment has raglan shaping for the sleeves and an attached I-cord front band with front button closure.

Body

With smaller cir needle and B, CO 180 (189, 207, 216, 234, 243, 261, 288) sts using the provisional cast-on method (see Techniques).

Beg with a WS row, work in St st for 6 rows.

TURNING ROW: (WS) Knit.

Change to larger cir needle.

NEXT ROW: (RS) Beg at the right edge of the chart with Row 1 of the *Cuff and Hem chart*, work first 9 (0, 9, 0, 9, 0, 9, 9) sts, rep next 27 sts 6 (7, 7, 8, 8, 9, 9, 10) times, then work 9 (0, 9, 0, 9, 0, 9, 9) sts at the left edge of the chart.

Work Rows 2–30 of the chart as established.

Change to smaller cir needle and A.

NEXT ROW: (RS) K45 (47, 52, 54, 58, 61, 65, 72), place marker (pm) for right

side, k90 (95, 103, 108, 118, 121, 131, 144), pm for left side, k45 (47, 52, 54, 58, 61, 65, 72).

Purl 1 WS row.

SHAPE WAIST
Sizes 31 (42)" (79 [106.5] cm) only
SET-UP ROW: (RS) Knit to m, sm, k1, k2tog (k3tog), knit to 3 sts before m, ssk, k1, sm, knit to end—178 (240) sts rem.

Work 3 rows even.

Sizes 33 (34¾, 46¼)" (84 [88.5, 117.5] cm) only
SET-UP ROW: (RS) Knit to 3 st before m, ssk, k1, sm, k1, k3tog, knit to 3 sts before m, ssk, k1, sm, k1, k2tog, knit to end—184 (202, 256) sts rem.

Work 3 rows even.

All sizes
NEXT (DEC) ROW: *Knit to 3 sts before m, ssk, k1, sm, k1, k2tog; rep from * once more, knit to end—4 sts dec'd.

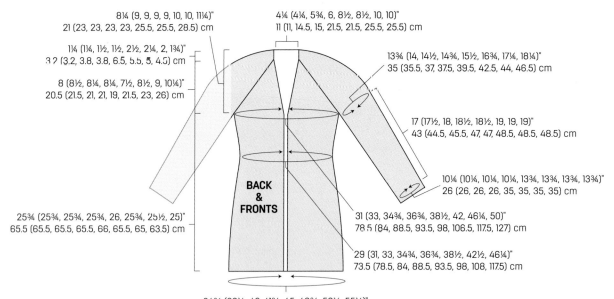

8¼ (9, 9, 9, 9, 10, 10, 11¼)"
21 (23, 23, 23, 23, 25.5, 25.5, 28.5) cm

1¼ (1¼, 1½, 1½, 2½, 2¼, 2, 1¾)"
3.2 (3.2, 3.8, 3.8, 6.5, 5.5, 5, 4.5) cm

8 (8½, 8¼, 8¼, 7½, 8½, 9, 10¼)"
20.5 (21.5, 21, 21, 19, 21.5, 23, 26) cm

25¾ (25¾, 25¾, 25¾, 26, 25¾, 25½, 25)"
65.5 (65.5, 65.5, 65.5, 66, 65.5, 65, 63.5) cm

4¼ (4¼, 5¾, 6, 8½, 8½, 10, 10)"
11 (11, 14.5, 15, 21.5, 21.5, 25.5, 25.5) cm

13¾ (14, 14½, 14¾, 15½, 16¾, 17¼, 18¼)"
35 (35.5, 37, 37.5, 39.5, 42.5, 44, 46.5) cm

17 (17½, 18, 18½, 18½, 19, 19, 19)"
43 (44.5, 45.5, 47, 47, 48.5, 48.5, 48.5) cm

10¼ (10¼, 10¼, 10¼, 13¾, 13¾, 13¾, 13¾)"
26 (26, 26, 26, 35, 35, 35, 35) cm

31 (33, 34¾, 36¾, 38½, 42, 46¼, 50)"
78.5 (84, 88.5, 93.5, 98, 106.5, 117.5, 127) cm

29 (31, 33, 34¾, 36¾, 38½, 42½, 46¼)"
73.5 (78.5, 84, 88.5, 93.5, 98, 108, 117.5) cm

34¾ (36½, 40, 41¾, 45, 46¾, 50¼, 55¼)"
88.5 (92.5, 101.5, 106, 114.5, 118.5, 127.5, 140.5) cm

BACK & FRONTS

Rep Dec row every 10 (12, 10, 8, 8, 8, 8, 8) rows 6 (5, 7, 8, 4, 9, 8, 5) more times, then every 0 (0, 0, 0, 6, 0, 0, 6) rows 0 (0, 0, 0, 6, 0, 0, 6) times—150 (160, 170, 180, 190, 200, 220, 240) sts rem; 38 (40, 43, 45, 47, 51, 55, 60) sts for each front, and 74 (80, 84, 90, 96, 98, 110, 120) sts for the back.

Work even until the piece measures 17¼ (17¼, 17¼, 17¼, 17½, 17¼, 17, 16½)" (44 [44, 44, 44, 44.5, 44, 43, 42] cm) from the turning row, ending with a WS row.

Change to the larger cir needle. Work Rows 1–20 of the **Waist chart**. Cut D.

Change to the smaller cir needle. Rejoin A and work 2 rows in St st.

SHAPE BUST

NEXT (INC) ROW: (RS) *Knit to 1 st before m, m1r, k1, sm, k1, m1l; rep from * once more, knit to end—4 sts inc'd.

Rep Inc row every 10 (10, 10, 10, 10, 8, 8, 8) rows 1 (1, 1, 1, 1, 3, 4, 4) more time(s)—158 (168, 178, 188, 198, 216, 240, 260) sts; 40 (42, 45, 47, 49, 55, 60, 65) sts for each front, and 78 (84, 88, 94, 100, 106, 120, 130) sts for the back.

Sizes 31 (34¾, 42)" (79 [88.5, 106.5] cm) only

Work 9 (9, 5) rows even.

NEXT (INC) ROW: (RS) Knit to m, sm, k1, m1l, knit to 1 st before marker, m1r, m1, sm, knit to end—160 (180, 218) sts; 40 (45, 55) sts for each front, and 80 (90, 108) sts for the back.

Sizes 33 (36¾, 38½)" (84 [93.5, 98] cm) only

Work 9 rows even.

NEXT (INC) ROW: (RS) Knit to 1 st before m, m1r, k1, sm, knit to m, sm, k1, m1l, knit to end—170 (190, 200) sts; 43 (48, 50) sts for each front, and 84 (94, 100) sts for the back.

All sizes
Cont even until the piece measures 25¾ (25¾, 25¾, 25¾, 26, 25¾, 25½, 25)" (65.5 [65.5, 65.5, 65.5, 66, 65.5, 65, 63.5] cm) from the turning row, ending with a RS row.

Armholes

NEXT ROW: (WS) *Knit to 4 (4, 4, 5, 5, 5, 6, 6) sts before the m, BO 8 (8, 8, 10, 10, 10, 12, 12) and remove m; rep from * once more, purl to end—144 (154, 164, 170, 180, 198, 216, 236) sts rem; 36 (39, 41, 43, 45, 50, 54, 59) sts for each front, and 72 (76, 82, 84, 90, 98, 108, 118) sts for the back. Set aside.

Sleeves

With smaller dpn and B, CO 54 (54, 54, 54, 72, 72, 72, 72) sts using the provisional cast-on method. Pm and join for working in rnds, being careful not to twist sts.

Knit 6 rnds.

TURNING RND: Purl.

Change to the larger dpn. Cont in St st (knit every rnd).

Sizes 31 (33, 34¾, 36¾)" (79 [84, 85.5, 93.5] cm) only
NEXT RND: Beg at the patt rep, work 27-st rep of Row 1 of the *Cuff and Hem chart* twice

Sizes 38½ (42, 46¼, 50)" (98 [106.5, 117.5, 127] cm) only
NEXT RND: Beg at the right edge of the Cuff and Hem chart, work Row 1 as foll, work first 9 sts, rep next 27 sts twice, then work 9 sts at left edge of chart.

All sizes
Work Rnds 2–30 as established. Cut D.

Change to the smaller dpn. Join A. Knit 1 rnd.

INC RND: K1, m1l, knit to last st, m1r, k1—2 sts inc'd.

Rep Inc rnd every 10 (9, 8, 8, 22, 13, 11, 11) rnds 8 (9, 10, 11, 4, 7, 8, 11) more times—72 (74, 76, 78, 82, 88, 90, 96) sts.

Cont even until the piece measures 17 (17½, 18, 18½, 18½, 19, 19, 19)" (43 [44.5, 45.5, 47, 47, 48.5, 48.5, 48.5] cm) from the turning rnd, ending the last rnd 4 (4, 4, 5, 5, 5, 6, 6) sts before the end of the rnd.

NEXT RND: BO 8 (8, 8, 10, 10, 10, 12, 12) sts, knit to the end—64 (66, 68, 68, 72, 78, 78, 84) sts rem.

JOIN BODY AND SLEEVES
With RS facing, k36 (39, 41, 43, 45, 50, 54, 59) right front sts, pm, k64 (66, 68, 68, 72, 78, 78, 84) sleeve sts, pm, k72 (76, 82, 84, 90, 98, 108, 118) back sts, pm, k64 (66, 68, 68, 72, 78, 78, 84) sleeve sts, pm, k36 (39, 41, 43, 45, 50, 54, 59) left front sts—272 (286, 300, 306, 324, 354, 372, 404) sts.

Yoke

Work 3 rows even in St st.

Note: Shaping the raglan armholes and front neck takes place at the same time. Read through the next instructions carefully before continuing.

RAGLAN DEC ROW: (RS) *Knit to 3 sts before m, ssk, k1, sm, k1, k2tog, rep from * 3 more times, knit to the end—8 sts dec'd for raglan.

NEXT ROW: Purl.

RAGLAN AND NECK DEC ROW: K1, ssk, *knit to 3 sts before m, ssk, k1, sm, k1, k2tog; rep from * 3 more times, knit to last 3 sts, k2tog, k1—10 sts dec'd; 2 neck sts, and 8 raglan sts.

NEXT ROW: Purl.

Rep the last 4 rows 6 (5, 6, 6, 9, 10, 11, 11) more times.

Size 38½" (98 cm) only
Rep the raglan and neck dec row every RS row 2 more times.

All sizes
Rep Raglan Dec row every RS row 11 (15, 12, 12, 1, 5, 4, 9) more time(s)—58 (58, 78, 84, 116, 116, 124, 116) sts rem; 4 (6, 8, 10, 10, 12, 14, 14) sts for each front, 14 (12, 16, 16, 26, 24, 22, 18) sts for each sleeve, and 22 (22, 30, 32, 44, 44, 52, 52) sts for the back.

Cut the yarn.

Attached i-cord band

With 2 dpn and B, CO 3 sts.

Knit 1 row, do not turn. Slide the sts to the right end of the dpn.

NEXT ROW: With RS of coat facing, beg at the right front hem edge, pull the yarn across the back of sts and k2; with left needle tip, pick up 1 st in the front edge, k2tog—3 sts. Do not turn. Slide the sts to the right end of the dpn.

Rep the last row in every row along the front edge to the bottom of the *Waist chart* patt.

*BUTTON LOOP: (Pull the yarn across the back of the sts, k3, do not turn and slide the sts to the right end of the dpn)

CUFF AND HEM CHART

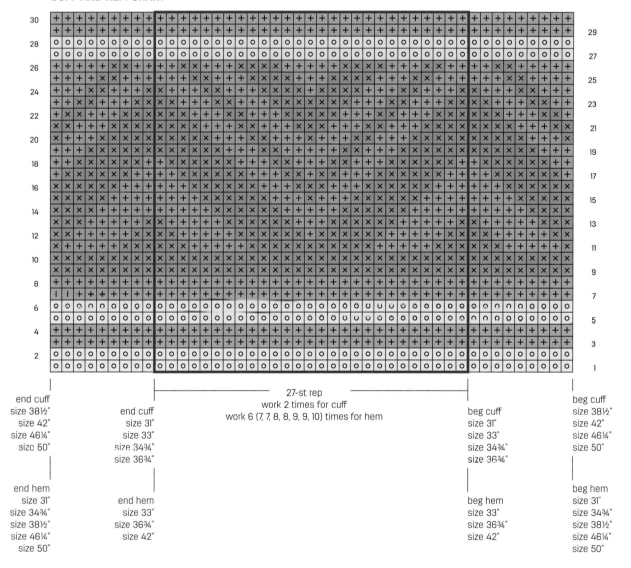

27-st rep
work 2 times for cuff
work 6 (7, 7, 8, 8, 9, 9, 10) times for hem

end cuff
size 38½"
size 42"
size 46¼"
size 50"

end cuff
size 31"
size 33"
size 34¾"
size 36¾"

beg cuff
size 31"
size 33"
size 34¾"
size 36¾"

beg cuff
size 38½"
size 42"
size 46¼"
size 50"

end hem
size 31"
size 34¾"
size 38½"
size 46¼"
size 50"

end hem
size 33"
size 36¾"
size 42"

beg hem
size 33"
size 36¾"
size 42"

beg hem
size 31"
size 34¾"
size 38½"
size 46¼"
size 50"

WAIST CHART

20	+	+	+	+	+	
	+	+	o	+	+	19
18	+	o	o	o	+	
	o	o	o	o	o	17
16	o	o	o	o	o	
	+	×	×	×	+	15
14	×	×	×	+	×	
	×	×	+	+	×	13
12	×	+	+	×	×	
	+	+	×	×	×	11
10	+	+	×	×	×	
	×	+	+	×	×	9
8	×	×	+	+	×	
	×	×	×	+	+	7
6	+	×	×	×	+	
	o	o	o	o	o	5
4	o	o	o	o	o	
	o	o	o	+	o	3
2	+	o	+	+	+	
	I	+	+	+	+	1

o	B
×	C
+	D
☐	pattern repeat

3 times. Skip the next 2 rows along the front edge.

NEXT ROW: Pull the yarn across the back of the sts, k2; with the left needle tip, pick up 1 st in the front edge, k2tog—3 sts. Do not turn. Slide the sts to the right end of the dpn.

Rep the last row 5 more times.

Rep from * 6 (6, 6, 6, 8, 8, 8) more times; the last button loop should be below the beg of the neck shaping.

Cont working the attached I-cord along the right front to the held neck sts.

TURN CORNER: (Pull the yarn across the back of the sts, k3, slide sts back to right end of dpn) twice.

Work in each of the held neck sts, turn the corner after the last of the held neck sts has been worked, then work

the attached I-cord in each row along the left front to the hem.

NEXT ROW: Pull the yarn across the back of the sts, and BO all sts.

Finishing

Weave in all the ends. Sew the under-arm seams. Fold the lower edges of the body to the WS along the turning row, sew to the inside. Fold the lower edges of the sleeves to the WS along the turning rnds, sew to the inside.

Allow the garment to soak in luke-warm water until thoroughly satu-rated. Gently press or spin out the excess water. Block to the measure-ments, pinning the hem, cuffs, and I-cord bands so they dry flat. Allow the garment to dry completely. Sew the buttons to the left front opposite the buttonholes.

The Native American people of the high desert decorated many of the neutral-colored sandstone rock formations around their dwelling spaces with graphic representations of things important to them. In this arid climate, many petroglyphs feature rain or storm motifs, but there are also animals and hunt-themed designs, as well as images representing the night sky, travel, dance, and various harvest ceremonies. Petroglyph National Monument just outside of Albuquerque, New Mexico, features a vast array of these carved images.

Petroglyph SOCKS

Finished Size
About 7¾ (8¾, 9¾)" (19.5 [22, 25] cm) foot circumference.

Project shown measures 7¾" (19.5 cm) circumference.

Yarn
Fingering weight (#1 Super Fine).

SHOWN HERE: Snowshoe Farm Alpacas Alpaca Blend fingering-weight yarn, (60% alpaca, 20% merino wool, 20% Tencel; 450 yd/4 oz [113g]); Fawn, 1 (1, 1) skein.

Needles
Size U.S. 1.5 (2.5 mm) set of 5 double-pointed (dpn).

Adjust needle size if necessary to obtain the correct gauge.

Notions
Markers (m); tapestry needle.

Gauge
33 sts and 41 rnds = 4" (10 cm) in St st after blocking; 32 sts and 53 rnds = 4" (10 cm) in chart patt, after blocking.

STITCH GUIDE

Stockinette Stitch *(worked in the rnd)*
ALL RNDS: Knit.

Design Notebook

These unisex socks are knit from the top (cuff) down, with a flap heel and a wide toe construction. The leg features knit/purl textured patterns taken from rain/lightning and spiral motifs found in petroglyphs in the American Southwest.

Leg

CO 64 (72, 80) sts loosely using long-tail cast-on method (see Techniques). Distribute sts evenly over 4 dpn with 16 (18, 20) sts on each needle. Place marker (pm) and join for working in rnds.

Size 7¾" (19.5 cm) only
RND 1: P2, *k2, p1, k2, p3; rep from * to last 6 sts, [k2, p1] twice.

Size 8¾" (22 cm) only
RND 1: *P1, k1, p3, k1; rep from *.

Size 9¾" (25 cm) only
RND 1: *P1, k2, p3, k2, p1, k3, p1, k2, p3, k2; rep from *.

All sizes
Rep Rnd 1 until piece measures about 2" (5 cm) from beg.

NEXT RND: Work Rnd 2 of appropriate chart for your size, working 16- (18-, 20-) st rep 4 times across rnd.

Work Rnds 3–60 (64, 71) of chart.

Heel

ROW 1: (RS) [Sl 1 wyb, k1] 16 (18, 20) times. Turn, leaving rem 32 (36, 40) sts on hold for instep.

ROW 2: (WS) Sl 1 wyf, p31 (35, 39), turn.

Rep Rows 1 and 2 until 32 (36, 40) rows have been worked.

TURNING THE HEEL

ROW 1: (RS) Sl 1 wyb, k18 (20, 22), ssk, k1, turn.

ROW 2: (WS) Sl 1 wyf, p7, p2tog, p1, turn.

ROW 3: Sl 1 wyb, knit to 1 st before gap, ssk, k1, turn.

ROW 4: Sl 1 wyf, purl to 1 st before gap, p2tog, p1, turn.

Rep Rows 3 and 4 until all sts have been worked, ending with a WS row, turn—20 (22, 24) sts rem.

Gusset

With RS facing, k20 (22, 24) heel sts, pick up and k16 (18, 20) sts along edge of heel flap, k32 (36, 40) instep sts, then pick up and k16 (18, 20) sts along rem edge of heel flap, k10 (11, 12)—84 (94, 104) sts. Pm and join to work in rnds; rnds beg at center of heel.

RND 1: K23 (26, 29), k2tog, pm, k34 (38, 42), pm, ssk, knit to end—2 sts dec'd.

SIZE LARGE CHART

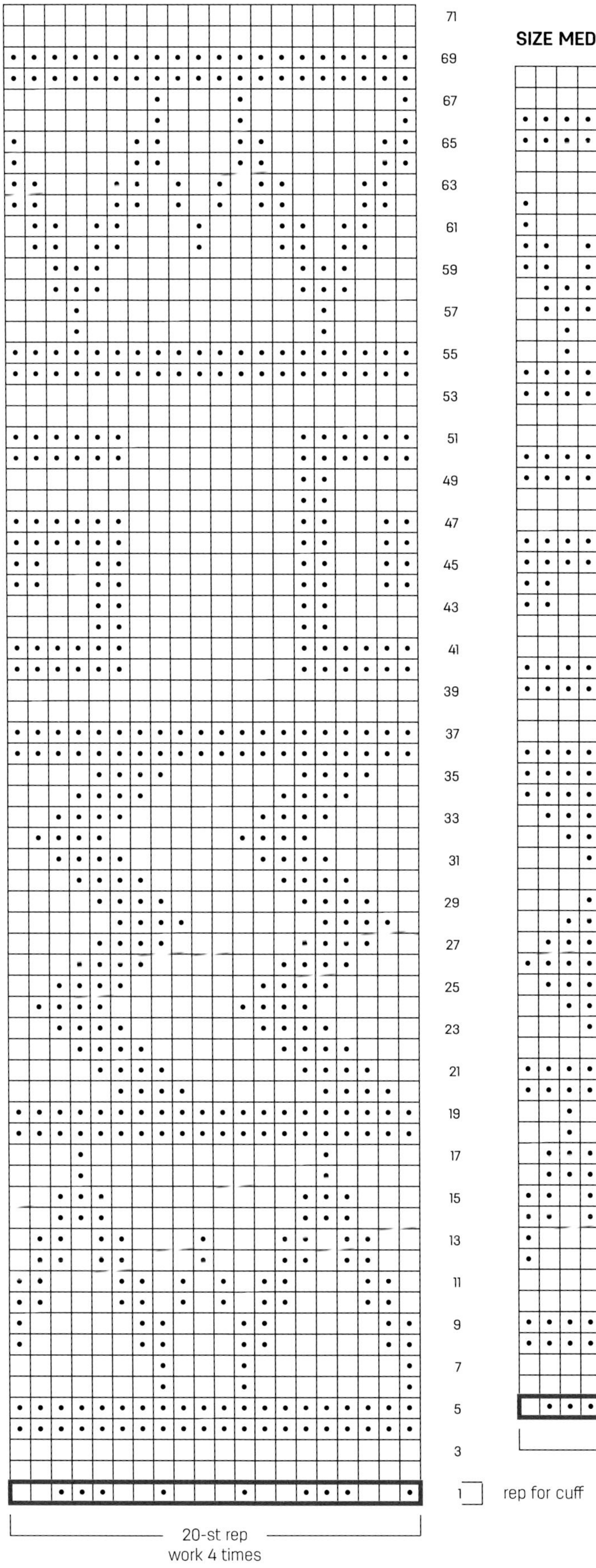

SIZE MEDIUM CHART

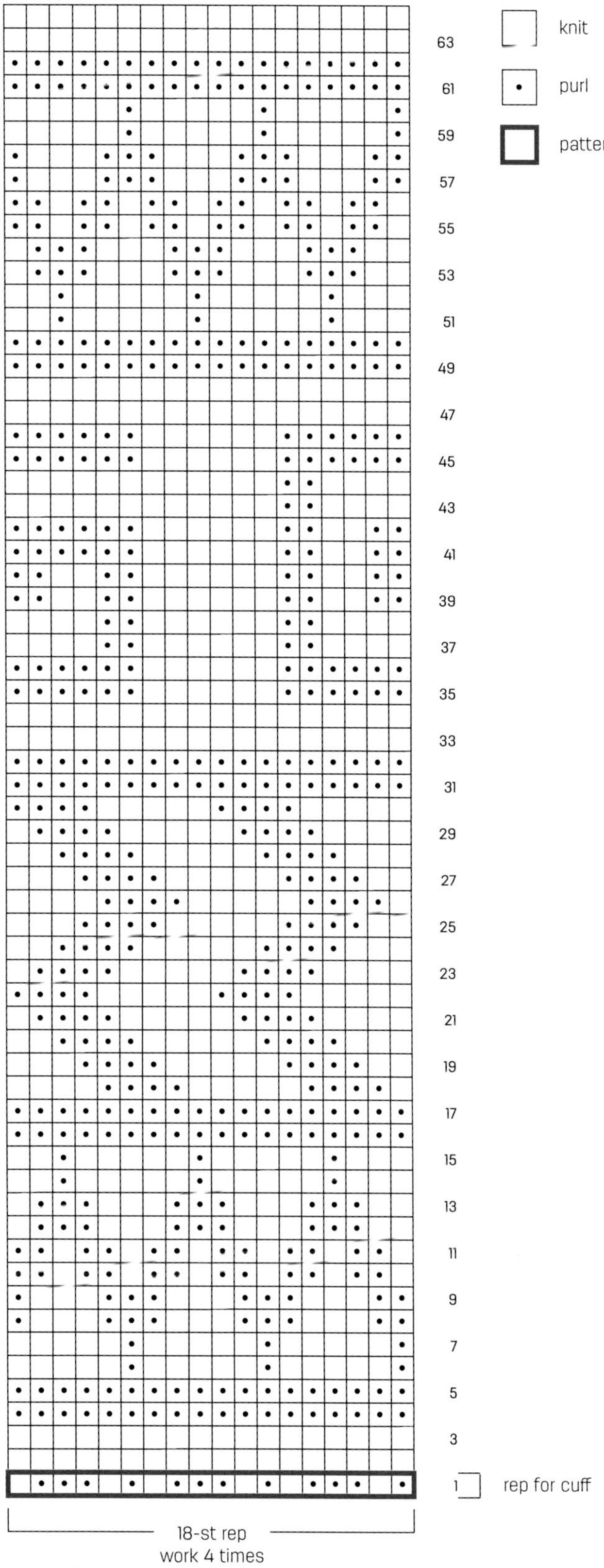

knit

• purl

pattern repeat

71
69
67
65
63
61
59
57
55
53
51
49
47
45
43
41
39
37
35
33
31
29
27
25
23
21
19
17
15
13
11
9
7
5
3

63
61
59
57
55
53
51
49
47
45
43
41
39
37
35
33
31
29
27
25
23
21
19
17
15
13
11
9
7
5
3
1

1 ⌐ rep for cuff

18-st rep
work 4 times

1 ⌐ rep for cuff

20-st rep
work 4 times

RND 2: Knit.

RND 3: Knit to 2 sts before m, k2tog, sm, knit to m, sm, ssk, knit to end—2 sts dec'd.

Rep last 2 rnds 8 (9, 10) more times—64 (72, 80) sts rem, with 16 (18, 20) sts on each dpn.

Cont even in St st until foot measures about 8 (9, 9½)" (20.5 [23, 24] cm) from heel, or 2¼ (2½, 3)" (5.5 [6.5, 7.5] cm) less than desired foot length.

Toe

DEC RND: Needle 1, knit to last 3 sts, k2tog, k1; Needle 2, k1, ssk, knit to end; Needle 3, knit to last 3 sts, k2tog, k1; Needle 4, k1, ssk, knit to end—4 sts dec'd.

NEXT RND: Knit.

Rep last 2 rnds 10 (12, 14) more times—20 sts rem.

NEXT RND: Knit 5 sts from Needle 1 and slip onto Needle 4, slip 5 sts from Needle 2 to Needle 3. Break yarn, leaving an 8" (20.5 cm) long tail. Thread tail onto tapestry needle and graft sts tog using the Kitchener st (see Techniques).

Finishing

Weave in all the loose ends. Soak the socks in lukewarm water until thoroughly saturated. Gently press or spin out the excess water. Lay the socks flat, patting into shape, but do not overly stretch. Allow the socks to dry completely.

SIZE SMALL CHART

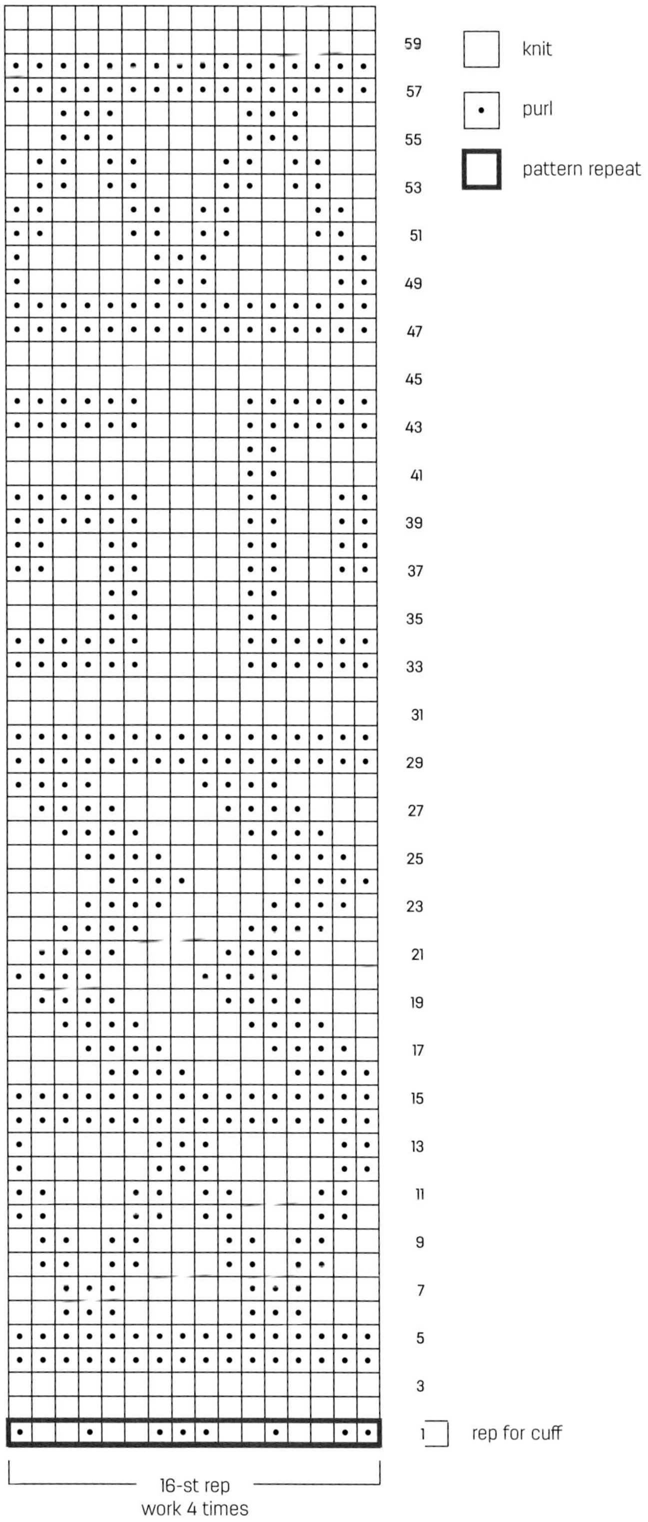

Row numbers (right side): 59, 57, 55, 53, 51, 49, 47, 45, 43, 41, 39, 37, 35, 33, 31, 29, 27, 25, 23, 21, 19, 17, 15, 13, 11, 9, 7, 5, 3, 1

Legend:
- ☐ knit
- • purl
- ▢ pattern repeat

rep for cuff

16-st rep
work 4 times

Ghost Ranch was the home of artist Georgia O'Keeffe in the mountains of northern New Mexico. Nestled against redrock cliff walls, this area was known to the Spanish explorers as "shining rock," and overlooks the waters of the Chama River as it flows southward. The ranch with its red and orange cliffs was the subject of many of O'Keeffe's paintings. The cattle skull marking the entrance to her property was also featured in several of her works and was the inspiration for the name of the ranch as well.

Ghost Ranch VEST

Finished Size
About 33¾ (36½, 37¾, 40½, 44½, 48½)" (85.5 [92.5, 96, 103, 113, 123] cm) bust circumference, including front bands, and 22½ (22½, 23¼, 24¼, 25, 25½)" (57 [57, 59, 61.5, 63.5, 65] cm) long.

Project shown measures 33¾" (85.5 cm).

Yarn
Sport weight (#2 Fine).

SHOWN HERE: Valley Yarns Northampton Sport (100% wool; 164 yd/1¾ oz [50 g]): Dark Gray (A), 6 (7, 7, 8, 8, 9) skeins; Lake Heather (B), 1 (2, 2, 3, 3, 3) skein(s); Rust (C), 1 (1, 2, 2, 3, 3) skein(s); Burgundy (D), 1 (1, 2, 2, 3, 3) skein(s); Eggplant (E), 1 (1, 2, 2, 3, 3) skein(s).

Needles
BODY: Size U.S. 4 (3.5 mm) 32" (80 cm) or longer circular (cir).

HEMS: Size U.S. 3 (3.25 mm) 32" (80 cm) or longer circular (cir) and set of 5 double-pointed (dpn).

ARMHOLE BANDS: Size U.S. 4 (3.5 mm) set of 5 double-pointed (dpn).

Adjust needle size if necessary to obtain the correct gauge.

Notions
Stitch markers (m); 5 stitch holders or waste yarn; tapestry needle; one 1½" (3.8 cm) clasp; sewing needle; sewing thread.

Gauge
24 sts and 32 rows = 4" (10 cm) over St st and Waist Chart on larger needles after blocking.

NOTE: If your gauge is slightly different for the colorwork sections, try going up one needle size to ensure gauge matches.

STITCH GUIDE

Garter Stitch *(worked back and forth, over any number of sts)*
ALL ROWS: Knit.

Stockinette Stitch *(worked back and forth, over any number of sts)*
ROW 1: (RS) Knit.

ROW 2: (WS) Purl.

Rep Rows 1 and 2 for patt.

Design Notebook

This women's vest is worked from the bottom hem up. It features a colorwork band of geometric motifs at the waist, and is finished with a shallow V-shaped front neckband in a diamond colorwork pattern. All facings are worked with a multicolored stripe pattern.

Body

With smaller cir needle and A, use the provisional cast-on method (see Techniques) to CO 48 (51, 54, 57, 63, 69) sts, place marker (pm), CO 97 (107, 109, 119, 131, 143) sts, pm, CO 48 (51, 54, 57, 63, 69) sts—193 (209, 217, 233, 257, 281) sts. Do not join.

NEXT ROW: (WS) Purl.

Cont in St st and work 2 rows with B, 2 rows with C, 2 rows with E, then 2 rows with D.

Change to A.

NEXT ROW: (RS) Knit.

TURNING ROW: (WS) Knit.

Change to larger cir needle. Cont in St st, slipping first st of every row until piece measures 3½ (3½, 3½, 3½, 3¾, 3¾)" (9 [9, 9, 9, 9.5, 9.5] cm) from turning row, ending with a WS row.

Work Rows 1–27 of **Waist chart**, making sure to knit or purl the first st in patt every row. Cut D.

Change to A. Cont in St st, slipping first st of every row until piece measures 14 (14, 14½, 15, 15¼, 15½)" (35.5 [35.5 37, 38, 38.5, 39.5] cm) from turning row, ending with a RS row.

DIVIDE FOR FRONT AND BACK

NEXT ROW: (WS) *Purl to 5 (5, 5, 6, 6, 7) sts before m, BO 10 (10, 10, 12, 12, 14) sts removing m; rep from * once more, purl to end—43 (46, 49, 51, 57, 62) sts rem for each front and 87 (97, 99, 107, 119, 129) sts rem for the back.

Right Front

SHAPE ARMHOLE

NEXT ROW: (RS) Sl 1 wyb, knit to end.

NEXT ROW: (WS) BO 1 st, purl to end—1 st dec'd.

Rep last 2 rows 4 (4, 5, 6, 6, 7) more times—38 (41, 43, 44, 50, 54) sts rem.

SHAPE NECK

DEC ROW 1: (RS) Sl 1 wyb, ssk, knit to end—1 st dec'd.

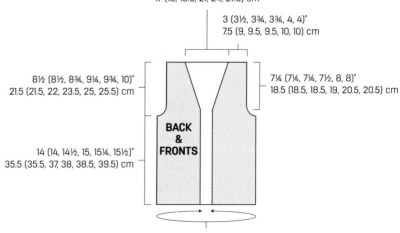

6¾ (7½, 7¼, 8¼, 9½, 10¾)"
17 (19, 18.5, 21, 24, 27.5) cm

3 (3½, 3¾, 3¾, 4, 4)"
7.5 (9, 9.5, 9.5, 10, 10) cm

8½ (8½, 8¾, 9¼, 9¾, 10)"
21.5 (21.5, 22, 23.5, 25, 25.5) cm

7¼ (7¼, 7¼, 7½, 8, 8)"
18.5 (18.5, 18.5, 19, 20.5, 20.5) cm

BACK & FRONTS

14 (14, 14½, 15, 15¼, 15½)"
35.5 (35.5, 37, 38, 38.5, 39.5) cm

31¾ (34½, 35¾, 38½, 42½, 46½)"
80.5 (87.5, 91, 98, 108, 118) cm,
plus 2" (5 cm) front opening

NEXT ROW: (WS) Sl 1 wyf, purl to end.

Rep last 2 rows 9 (9, 10, 11, 13, 15) more times—28 (31, 32, 32, 36, 38) sts rem.

DEC ROW 2: (RS) Sl 1 wyb, k2tog, knit to end—1 st dec'd.

NEXT ROW: (WS) Sl 1 wyf, purl to end.

Rep last 2 rows 9 (9, 9, 9, 11, 13) more times—18 (21, 22, 22, 24, 24) sts rem.

Cont even until armhole measures 8½ (8½, 8¾, 9¼, 9¾, 10)" (21.5 [21.5, 22, 23.5, 25, 25.5] cm). Place rem sts on holder.

Back

Rejoin A to beg with a RS row.

Cont in St st and BO 1 st at beg of next 10 (10, 12, 14, 14, 16) rows—77 (87, 87, 93, 105, 113) sts rem.

Cont even, slipping first st of every row until armhole measures 8½ (8½, 8¾, 9¼, 9¾, 10)" (21.5 [21.5, 22, 23.5, 25, 25.5] cm), ending with a WS row. Place first 18 (21, 22, 22, 24, 24) sts on holder for right shoulder, center 41 (45, 43, 49, 57, 65) sts on second holder for back neck, and place rem 18 (21, 22, 22, 24, 24) sts on third holder for left shoulder.

Left Front

SHAPE ARMHOLE

Rejoin A to beg with a RS row.

NEXT ROW: (RS) BO 1 st, knit to end—1 st dec'd.

NEXT ROW: (WS) Sl 1 wyf, purl to end.

Rep last 2 rows 4 (4, 5, 6, 6, 7) more times—38 (41, 43, 44, 50, 54) sts rem.

SHAPE NECK

DEC ROW 1: (RS) Knit to last 3 sts, k2tog, k1—1 st dec'd.

NEXT ROW: (WS) Sl 1 wyf, purl to end.

Rep last 2 rows 9 (9, 10, 11, 13, 15) more times—28 (31, 32, 32, 36, 38) sts rem.

DEC ROW 2: (RS) Knit to last 3 sts, ssk, k1—1 st dec'd.

NEXT ROW: (WS) Sl 1 wyf, purl to end.

Rep last 2 rows 9 (9, 9, 9, 11, 13) more times—18 (21, 22, 22, 24, 24) sts rem.

Cont even until armhole measures 8½ (8½, 8¾, 9¼, 9¾, 10)" (21.5 [21.5, 22, 23.5, 25, 25.5] cm).

JOIN SHOULDERS

Place 18 (21, 22, 22, 24, 24) held left back shoulder sts on dpn. Join shoulder using the three-needle bind-off (see Techniques).

Join the right shoulder sts in the same way as the left.

Neckband

With larger cir needle and A, beg at turning row at bottom of right front, pick up and k18 (18, 18, 18, 19, 19) sts along right front to bottom of color-work band (about 1 st in each sl st),

WAIST CHART

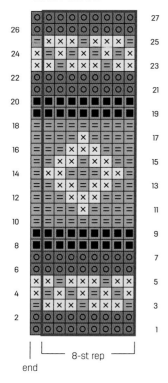

27

26
25

24
23

22
21

20
19

18
17

16
15

14
13

12
11

10
9

8
7

6
5

4
3

2
1

| 8-st rep |
end

BORDER CHART

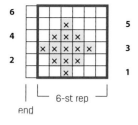

6
5

4
3

2
1

| 6-st rep |
end

Key:

☐ A

☒ B

= C

◉ D

■ E

☐ pattern repeat

---

18 sts along edge of colorwork band, 85 (83, 87, 90, 91, 93) evenly along right front to shoulder seam, knit held 41 (45, 43, 49, 57, 65) back neck sts, pick up and k85 (86, 87, 90, 91, 93) sts along left front to top of colorwork band, 18 sts along edge of colorwork band, then 18 (18, 18, 18, 19, 19) sts evenly along front edge to turning row at bottom of left front—283 (283, 289, 301, 313, 325) sts. Do not join.

Purl 1 WS row.

Work Rows 1–6 of **Border chart**.

With A only, knit 2 rows (second row forms turning row).

Change to smaller cir needle. Work 2 rows in St st.

Cont in St st, work 2 rows with B, 2 rows with C, 2 rows with E.

Change to A. Knit 1 row. BO all sts loosely pwise.

Armhole Bands

With larger dpn and A, beg at center of underarm, pick up and k103 (103, 109, 115, 121, 121) sts evenly around armhole. Pm and join for working in rnds.

Knit 1 rnd.

Work Rows 1–6 of **Border chart**.

With A, knit 1 rnd, then purl 1 rnd for turning rnd.

Change to smaller dpn. Knit 2 rnds.

Cont in St st, knit 2 rnds with B, 2 rnds with C, 2 rnds with E, then 2 rnds with D.

BO all sts loosely.

Finishing

Remove the provisional CO at the bottom edge. Turn the hem to the WS along the turning row. With A threaded in tapestry needle, graft sts to the WS. Turn the neckband to the WS along the turning row. With D, sew the BO edge of the neckband to the WS. Turn the armhole bands to the WS along the turning rnd. With D, sew the BO edge to the WS.

Weave in all the loose ends. Allow the garment to soak in lukewarm water until thoroughly saturated. Gently press or spin out the excess water. Block to the measurements, pinning the hems so that they dry flat. Allow the garment to dry completely. Using sewing needle and thread, sew the clasp to the front edges centering the clasp on the **Waist chart** patt.

The Three Sisters is a traditional Native American method of planting crops. The corn is planted in the center; beans are allowed to use the stalks as climbing trellises, and squash or pumpkin plant vines keep the roots of these plants cool during the hot summers. All three of these plants were grown as staples in the Native culture's diet.

Finished Size
About 51½" (131 cm) wide and 18" (45.5 cm) long at center.

Yarn
Fingering weight (#1 Super Fine).

SHOWN HERE: The Woolen Rabbit Lucent (70% merino/20% cashmere/10% nylon; 410 yd/4 oz [115 g]): Butterscotch, 3 skeins.

Needles
BODY: Size U.S. 5 (3.75 mm) 32" (80 cm) or longer circular (cir).

BORDER: Two size U.S. 5 (3.75 mm) double-pointed needles (dpn) for Pumpkin Vine border.

Adjust needle size if necessary to obtain the correct gauge.

Notions
Stitch markers (m); cable needle (cn); tapesry needle.

Gauge
21 sts and 32 rows = 4" (10 cm) in Corn Ears chart, after blocking.

STITCH GUIDE

1/1 LPT (1 OVER 1 LEFT PURL TWIST): Sl 1 st to cn and hold in front of work, p1, k1 from cn.

1/1 RPT (1 OVER 1 RIGHT PURL TWIST): Sl 1 st to cn and hold in back of work, k1, p1 from cn.

2/1 LC (2 OVER 1 LEFT CROSS): Sl 2 sts to cn and hold in front of work, k1, k2 from cn.

2/1 RC (2 OVER 1 RIGHT CROSS): Sl 1 st to cn and hold in back of work, k2, k1 from cn.

2/1 LPC (2 OVER 1 LEFT PURL CROSS): Sl 2 sts to cn and hold in front of work, p1, k2 from cn.

2/1 RPC (2 OVER 1 RIGHT PURL CROSS): Sl 1 st to cn and hold in back of work, k2, p1 from cn.

S2KP: Sl 2 sts together as if to knit 2 together, knit 1, pass slipped stitch over—2 sts dec'd.

SSSP: Holding yarn in front, slip 3 sts individually knitwise, then slip these 3 sts back onto left needle tip (they will be twisted on the needle), and purl them together through their back loops—2 sts dec'd.

Notes

The first 3 and last 3 sts of each row are worked in garter stitch (knit every row) and do not appear on the charts.

The charts are worked back and forth. Read the right-side (odd-numbered) rows from right to left and the wrong-side (even-numbered) rows from left to right.

Shawl

With cir needle, CO 85 sts loosely using the long-tail cast-on method (see Techniques).

Knit 3 rows.

SET-UP ROW: (RS) K3, place marker (pm), (k9, pm, k26, pm) twice, k9, pm, k3.

NEXT ROW: K3, purl to last 3 sts slipping m as you come to them, k3.

NEXT ROW: K3, sm, work (Row 1 of *Corn Ears chart A* over next 9 sts, sm, Row 1 of *Bean Vine chart* over next 26 sts, sm) twice, Row 1 of *Corn Ears chart A* over next 9 sts, sm, k3.

NEXT ROW: K3, sm, work (Row 2 of *Corn Ears chart A* over next 9 sts, sm, Row 2 of *Bean Vine chart* over next 26 sts, sm) twice, Row 2 of *Corn Ears chart A* over next 9 sts, sm, k3.

Work Rows 3–48 of *Corn Ears chart A*, and Rows 2–26 of *Bean Vine chart*, then rep 26 rows of chart as needed—223 sts.

NEXT ROW: (RS) K3, sm, work (Row 1 of *Corn Ears chart B* to next m, sm, next row of *Bean Vine chart* over next 26 sts, sm) twice, Row 1 of *Corn Ears chart B* to next m, sm, k3—6 sts inc'd.

Work Rows 2–40 of *Corn Ears chart B*, working *Bean Vine chart* as established—343 sts.

NEXT ROW: (RS) K3, sm, work (Row 9 of *Corn Ears chart A* to next m, sm, next row of *Bean Vine chart* over next 26 sts, sm) twice, Row 9 of *Corn Ears chart A* to next m, sm, k3—6 sts inc'd.

Design Notebook

This shawl is constructed from the neck down in a three-quarter circle shape. It features three panels (at the left and right front and center back) of a simple corn-ears lace pattern. Eyelet increases worked at the edges of these panels shape the shawl. In addition, there are two narrow panels of a runner bean leaf lace that run vertically up the shawl. Once the body of the shawl has been worked, the pumpkin vine and eyelet edging is knitted on.

□ k on RS; p on WS		↓3 (k1, p1, k1) in same st
• p on RS; k on WS		‖‖ k3 on RS; p3 on WS
ℒ k1 tbl on RS; p1 tbl on WS		⌒ BO
○ yo		▨ no stitch
╱ k2tog on RS; p2tog on WS		◤◢ 1/1 RPT (see Stitch Guide)
╲ ssk		◣◥ 1/1 LPT (see Stitch Guide)
⋏ k3tog		◸◿ 2/1 RC (see Stitch Guide)
⋋ sssp (see Stitch Guide)		◺◹ 2/1 LC (see Stitch Guide)
⋏ s2kp (see Stitch Guide)		◤◢ 2/1 RPC (see Stitch Guide)
V sl 1 wyf on WS		◣◥ 2/1 LPC (see Stitch Guide)

CORN EARS CHART A

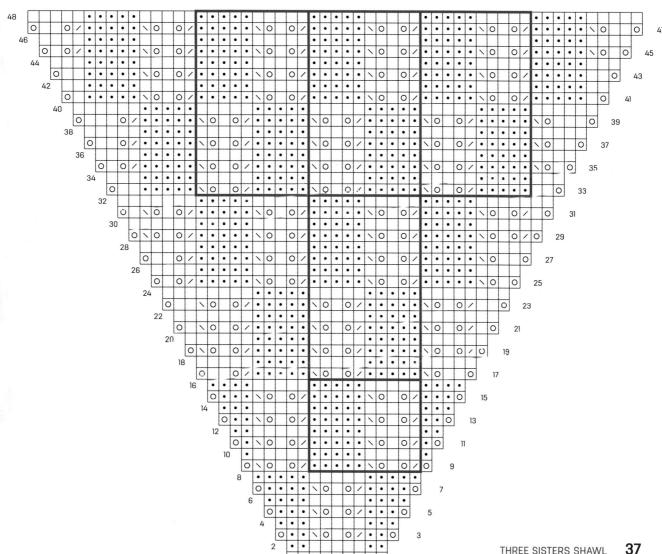

CORN EARS CHART B

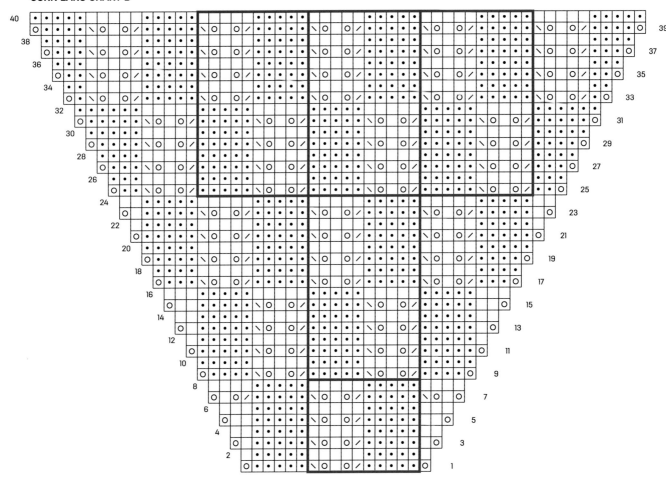

	k on RS; p on WS			⌄3	(k1, p1, k1) in same st
•	p on RS; k on WS			‖‖	k3 on RS; p3 on WS
Ω	k1 tbl on RS; p1 tbl on WS			⌒	BO
O	yo				no stitch
∕	k2tog on RS; p2tog on WS			⟋⟍	1/1 RPT (see Stitch Guide)
⟍	ssk			⟍⟋	1/1 LPT (see Stitch Guide)
⋌	k3tog			⟋⟍	2/1 RC (see Stitch Guide)
⋊	sssp (see Stitch Guide)			⟍⟋	2/1 LC (see Stitch Guide)
⋀	s2kp (see Stitch Guide)			⟋⟍	2/1 RPC (see Stitch Guide)
V	sl 1 wyf on WS			⟍⟋	2/1 LPC (see Stitch Guide)

	k on RS; p on WS
•	p on RS; k on WS
ℓ	k1 tbl on RS; p1 tbl on WS
o	yo
/	k2tog on RS; p2tog on WS
\	ssk
⋏	k3tog
⋋	sssp (see Stitch Guide)
∧	s2kp (see Stitch Guide)
V	sl 1 wyf on WS
³	(k1, p1, k1) in same st
III	k3 on RS; p3 on WS
⌢	BO
▨	no stitch
◣	1/1 RPT (see Stitch Guide)
◢	1/1 LPT (see Stitch Guide)
▱	2/1 RC (see Stitch Guide)
▱	2/1 LC (see Stitch Guide)
▱	2/1 RPC (see Stitch Guide)
▱	2/1 LPC (see Stitch Guide)

PUMPKIN VINES BORDER

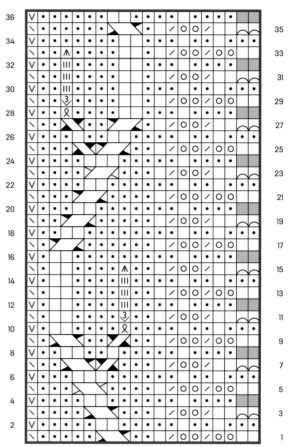

BEAN VINES CHART

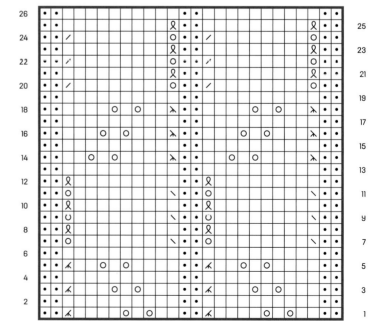

Work Rows 10–48 of **Corn Ears chart A**, working **Bean Vine chart** as established —463 sts.

Knit 2 rows even, removing m.

NEXT (INC) ROW: K1, [k1, yo] 3 times, [k2tog, yo] to last 3 sts, [k1, yo] twice, k1—468 sts.

Knit 2 rows even. Cut yarn.

Border

With dpn, CO 18 sts loosely using the long-tail cast-on method. Knit 1 row.

NEXT ROW: (RS) With RS facing, beg at one end of cir needle, work Row 1 of **Pumpkin Vines Border chart** over 17 border sts, knit together last st of border with first st of shawl—1 st shawl st dec'd. Turn.

NEXT ROW: (WS) Work Row 2 of **Pumpkin Vines Border** over border sts. Turn.

Work Rows 3–36 of chart as established, then rep Rows 1–36 until all shawl sts have been dec'd, ending with a WS row—18 sts rem.

BO rem border sts loosely kwise.

Finishing

Weave in all the loose ends leaving the ends to trim after blocking. Allow the shawl to soak in lukewarm water until thoroughly saturated. Gently press or spin out the excess water. Block the shawl to measurements, pinning out each point along the edge of the border. Allow the shawl to dry completely. Trim the loose ends.

Brimstone Gulch is one of the Southwest region's narrowest slot canyons, measuring no more than a yard wide at its broadest point, and sometimes completely impassible at only a few inches of width. Near Escalante, Utah, the slot canyons are extremely narrow, throwing the colored sandstone walls into dark and murky shadows, and lit only in occasional narrow shafts of sunlight from above.

Brimstone Gulch SWEATER

Finished Size

About 32 (34¼, 36¼, 39¼, 41½, 45¾, 48, 51¾)" (81.5 [87, 92, 99.5, 105.5, 116, 122, 131.5] cm) chest circumference, and 21¼ (21¾, 24¾, 25¼, 25½, 27, 27½, 27¾)" (54 [55, 63, 64, 65, 68.5, 70, 70.5] cm) long.

Project shown measures 45¾" (116 cm).

Yarn

DK weight (#3 Light).

SHOWN HERE: Rowan Felted Tweed DK (50% merino wool, 25% alpaca, 25% viscose; 191 yd [175 m]/1 ¾ oz [50 g]). #170 Seafarer (dark blue, A), 5 (5, 5, 6, 6, 7, 7, 8) skeins; #167 Maritime (blue-gray, B) 1 (1, 1, 1, 1, 1, 2, 2) skein(s); #160 Gilt (yellow, C) 1 (1, 1, 1, 1, 1, 2, 2) skein(s); #158 Pine (dark green, D) 1 (1, 1, 1, 1, 1, 2, 2) skein(s); #154 Ginger (rust, E) 1 (1, 1, 1, 1, 1, 2, 2) skein(s).

Needles

BODY: Size U.S. 5 (3.75 mm) 24 (60 cm) or longer circular (cir) and set of 5 double-pointed (dpn).

BODY HEM: Size U.S. 4 (3.5 mm) 24" (60 cm) or longer circular (cir) .

SLEEVES: Size U.S. 5 (3.75 mm) set of 5 double-pointed (dpn).

SLEEVE HEM: Size U.S. 4 (3.5 mm) set of 5 double-pointed (dpn).

Adjust needle size if necessary to obtain the correct gauge.

Notions

Stitch markers (m); waste yarn or stitch holders; tapestry needle.

Gauge

22 sts and 28 rows = 4 (10 cm) in St st in the round using larger needles, after blocking.

(See Notes below on maintaining gauge over colorwork yoke.)

Notes

The chart is worked in the round; chart rows are read from right to left.

Be sure to check your gauge over the colorwork chart, too. If your gauge changes over the colorwork sections of the yoke, you may wish to go up or down a needle size to maintain a consistent gauge throughout.

STITCH GUIDE

Sewn Bind-Off

Cut working yarn 2 yd (1.8 m) long and thread into tapestry needle. *Insert tapestry needle through first 2 stitches on left needle tip, from right to left, pull yarn through, leaving stitches on left-hand needle. Insert tapestry needle through the first stitch again, from front to back, pull yarn through and slip stitch off left needle tip. Repeat from * until all stitches have been bound off. Pull yarn through the last stitch and fasten securely on the wrong side.

Design Notebook

This project is a unisex/man's sweater with a boxy fit. The sweater is knitted in the round from the bottom to the armholes The sleeves are then knit in the round to the armholes and joined to the body. A multicolored yoke with concentric decreases to the neckband shapes the top of the garment.

Body

With smaller cir needle and B, CO 176 (188, 200, 216, 228, 252, 264, 284) sts using the provisional cast-on method (see Techniques). Place marker (pm) and join for working in rnds, being careful not to twist sts.

Knit 7 rnds. Change to A.

NEXT (TURNING) RND: Purl.

Change to larger cir needle.

Cont in St st (knit every rnd) until piece measures 15 (15½, 16, 16½, 16¾, 17, 17½, 17¾)" (38 [39.5, 40.5, 42, 42.5, 43, 44.5, 45] cm), or desired length from turning rnd, ending last rnd 4 (4, 5, 6, 6, 6, 7, 7) sts before end of rnd.

ARMHOLES

BO next 8 (8, 10, 12, 12, 12, 14, 14) sts for armhole, removing beg-of-rnd

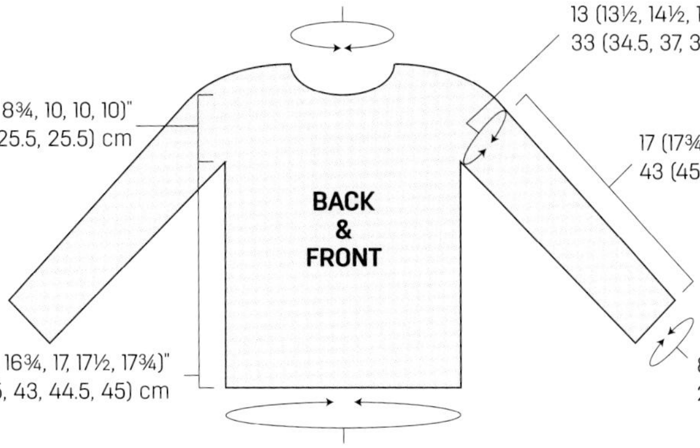

14¼ (15, 15¾, 16¼, 17, 17½, 18¼, 19¾)"
36 (38, 40, 41.5, 43, 44.5, 46.5, 50) cm

13 (13½, 14½, 15¼, 15¾, 16¼, 17½, 18½)"
33 (34.5, 37, 38.5, 40, 41.5, 44.5, 47) cm

6¼ (6¼, 8¾, 8¾, 8¾, 10, 10, 10)"
16 (16, 22, 22, 22, 25.5, 25.5, 25.5) cm

17 (17¾, 18, 18½, 19, 19½, 20, 21)"
43 (45, 45.5, 47, 48.5, 49.5, 51, 53.5) cm

BACK & FRONT

15 (15½, 16, 16½, 16¾, 17, 17½, 17¾)"
38 (39.5, 40.5, 42, 42.5, 43, 44.5, 45) cm

8¾ (9, 9½, 9½, 9¾, 9¾, 10¼, 11)"
22 (23, 24, 24, 25, 25, 26, 28) cm

32 (34¼, 36¼, 39¼, 41½, 45¾, 48, 51¾)"
81.5 (87, 92, 99.5, 105.5, 116, 122, 131.5) cm

m, knit until there are 80 (86, 90, 96, 102, 114, 118, 128) sts after BO gap for front, BO 8 (8, 10, 12, 12, 12, 14, 14) sts for armhole, then knit to end—80 (86, 90, 96, 102, 114, 118, 128) sts rem for each front and back. Set aside.

SLEEVES

With smaller dpn and B, CO 48 (50, 52, 52, 54, 54, 56, 60) sts using the provisional cast-on method. Pm and join for working in rnds, being careful not to twist sts.

Knit 7 rnds. Change to A.

NEXT (TURNING) RND: Purl.

Change to larger dpn. Knit 7 rnds.

INC RND: K1, m1l, knit to last st, m1r, k1—2 sts inc'd.

Knit 6 (6, 6, 5, 5, 5, 5, 5) rnds even.

Rep last 7 (7, 7, 6, 6, 6, 6, 6) rnds 10 (10, 12, 14, 14, 16, 18, 19) more times, then rep Inc rnd once more—72 (74, 80, 84, 86, 90, 96, 102) sts. Cont even in St st until piece measures 17 (17¾, 18, 18½, 19, 19½, 20, 21)" (43 [45, 45.5, 47, 48.5, 49.5, 51, 53.5] cm), or desired length from turning rnd, ending last rnd 4 (4,

5, 6, 6, 6, 7, 7) sts before end of rnd. BO 8 (8, 10, 12, 12, 12, 14, 14) sts, removing beg-of-rnd m—64 (66, 70, 72, 74, 78, 82, 88) sts rem.

JOIN BODY AND SLEEVES

With larger cir needle and A, k64 (66, 70, 72, 74, 78, 82, 88) sts for left sleeve, k80 (86, 90, 96, 102, 114, 118, 128) sts for front, k64 (66, 70, 72, 74, 78, 82, 88) sts for right sleeve, then k80 (86, 90, 96, 102, 114, 118, 128) sts for back—288 (304, 320, 336, 352, 384, 400, 428) sts. Pm for beg-of-rnd and join for working in rnds. Change to larger dpn when there are too few sts rem to work comfortably on cir needle.

Knit 4 rnds even. Cut A.

Yoke

Work Rows 1–18 of *Yoke chart*. Change to A and knit 3 rnds.

DEC RND 1: *K2, k2tog; rep from * —216 (228, 240, 252, 264, 288, 300, 324) sts rem.

NEXT RND: Knit and dec 0 (4, 0, 4, 0, 0, 4, 4) sts evenly spaced around —216

(224, 240, 248, 264, 288, 296, 320) sts rem. Cut A.

Sizes 32 (34¼)" (81.5 [87] cm) only
Work Rows 1–9 of *Yoke chart*.

Sizes 36¼ (39¼, 41½, 45¾, 48, 51¾)" (92 [99.5, 105.5, 116, 122, 131.5] cm) only
Work Rows 1–18 of *Yoke chart*.

All sizes
Change to A and knit 2 rnds.

Sizes 34¼ (39¼, 48, 51¾)" (87 [99.5, 122, 131.5] cm) only
DEC RND 2: K4, *[k2tog, k1]; rep from * to last 4 sts, k4 —152 (168, 200, 216) sts rem.

Sizes 32 (36¼, 41½, 45¾)" (81.5 [92, 105.5, 116] cm) only
DEC RND 2: *K1, k2tog; rep from *—144 (160, 176, 192) sts rem.

All sizes
Knit 2 rnds even.

Sizes 32 (34¼)" (81.5 [87] cm) only
DEC RND 3: K6, *k2tog; rep from * to last 6 sts, k6—78 (82) sts rem.

YOKE CHART

17
15
13
11
9
7
5
3
1

4-st rep

◆ B

ı C

○ D

• E

□ pattern repeat

Sizes 36¼ (39¼, 41½)" (91.5 [99.5 105.5] cm) only

Work Rows 1–9 of **Yoke chart**.

Change to A and knit 2 rnds.

DEC RND 3: K6, *k2tog; rep from * to last 6 sts, k6—86 (90, 94) sts rem.

Sizes 45¾ (48, 51¾)" (116 [122, 131.5] cm) only

Change to A and knit 2 rnds.

DEC RND 3: *K2tog; rep from *—96 (100, 108) sts rem.

ALL SIZES

Knit 8 (10, 10, 10, 10, 10, 10, 10) rnds even. BO all sts using sewn bind-off method (see Stitch Guide).

Finishing

Remove the provisional CO and place the resulting sts on a smaller cir needle. Turn the hem to the WS along the turn rnd. Using tapestry needle threaded with length of A, whipstitch live sts from WS of the garment. Sew the underarm seams.

Weave in all the loose ends. Allow the garment to soak in lukewarm water until thoroughly saturated. Gently press or spin out the excess water. Block the garment to measurements. Allow the garment to dry completely.

Just north of Flagstaff, Arizona, the Arizona Snow Bowl features tons of great skiing. With 2,300 feet of drop on the trails, these challenging runs can be seen crisscrossing down the gray mountain sides from miles away. Even in the middle of summer, the top of Agassiz Peak, at an elevation of 12,360 feet, often has snow, and year-round visitors can get incredible scenic views of the Kachina Peaks Wilderness area from the ski-hill tram.

Snow Bowl HOODIE

Finished Size
About 38 (39, 41, 42¾, 44¼, 47½, 50¼, 54)" (96.5 [99, 104, 108.5, 112.5, 120.5, 127.5, 137] cm) bust circumference, and 23¼ (23½, 24½, 25, 25¾, 26½, 27, 27½)" (59 [59.5, 62, 63.5, 65.6, 67.5, 68.5, 70] cm) long from neck at center back.

Project shown measures 41" (104 cm).

Yarn
DK, Light Worsted (#3 Light).

SHOWN HERE: Green Mountain Spinnery New Mexico Organic (100% fine wool; 180 yd/2 oz [57 g]): Grey 10 (10, 10, 11, 11, 12, 12,13) skeins.

Needles
BODY: Size U.S. 5 (3.75 mm) 32" (80 cm) or longer circular (cir).

SLEEVES: Size U.S. 5 (3.75 mm) double-pointed (dpn).

Adjust needle size if necessary to obtain the correct gauge.

Notions
Stitch markers (m); cable needle (cn); stitch holders or waste yarn; tapestry needle; zipper to fit length from bottom hem to top of front neckband; sewing needle; matching sewing thread.

Gauge
20 sts and 29 rows = 4" (10 cm) in St st, after blocking;

15-st Moguls Cable panel = about 2" (5 cm) wide, after blocking;

66-st Ski Run Cable panel = 9" (23 cm) wide, after blocking.

STITCH GUIDE

Stockinette Stitch (worked back and forth over any number of sts):

ROW 1: (RS) Knit.

ROW 2: (WS) Purl.

Rep Rows 1 and 2 for patt.

Stockinette Stitch (worked in the round over any number of sts)

ALL RNDS: Knit.

1/1 LC (1 OVER 1 LEFT CROSS): Slip 1 st to cn and hold in front, k1, k1 from cn.

1/1 RC (1 OVER 1 RIGHT CROSS): Slip 1 st to cn and hold in back, k1, k1 from cn.

2/2 LC (2 OVER 2 LEFT CROSS): Slip 2 sts to cn and hold in front, k2, k2 from cn.

2/2 LPC (2 OVER 2 LEFT PURL CROSS): Slip 2 sts to cn and hold in front, p2, k2 from cn.

2/2 RC (2 OVER 2 RIGHT CROSS): Slip 2 sts to cn and hold in back, k2, k2 from cn.

2/2 RPC (2 OVER 2 RIGHT PURL CROSS): Slip 2 sts to cn and hold in back, k2, p2 from cn.

3/3 RC (3 OVER 3 RIGHT CROSS): Slip 3 sts to cn and hold in back, k3, k3 from cn.

Notes

Both charts are worked back and forth for the body. Read the right-side (odd-numbered) rows from right to left and the wrong-side (even-numbered) rows from left to right. The Moguls chart is worked in the round for the sleeves. Read all rows from right to left.

The front edges have two edge sts used to sew in the zipper. Slip the first stitch of each row to help create a smooth edge.

A circular needle is used for the body to accommodate the large number of stitches. Do not join, work back and forth.

Body

With cir needle, CO 202 (208, 218, 226, 234, 250, 264, 282) sts using the long-tail cast-on method (see Techniques). Do not join.

NEXT ROW: (WS) P2 (edge sts), place marker (pm), p2, k2, p4, [k2, p2] 10 (10, 11, 11, 12, 13, 14, 15) times, k0 (2, 0, 2, 0, 0, 0, 0), pm for left side, [k2, p2] 4 (4, 5, 6, 6, 7, 8, 9) times, k2 (3, 2, 0, 2, 2, 1, 2), pm, p2, k2, [p4, k2] twice, p2, k4, [p2, k2] 5 times, p2, k4, p2, k2, [p4, k2] twice, p2, pm, [k2, p2] 4 (4, 5, 6, 6, 7, 8, 9) times, k2 (3, 2, 0, 2, 2, 1, 2), pm for right side, p0 (2, 0, 2, 0, 0, 0, 0), [p2, k2] 10 (10, 11, 11, 12, 13, 14, 15) times, p4, k2, p2, pm, p2 edge sts.

Slipping m as you come to them, work 18 more rows in established ribbing, ending with a WS row.

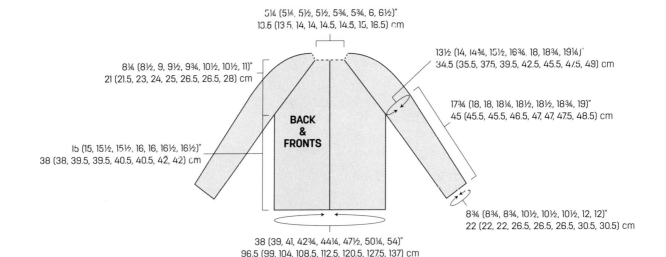

5¼ (5¼, 5½, 5½, 5¾, 5¾, 6, 6½)"
13.5 (13.5, 14, 14, 14.5, 14.5, 15, 16.5) cm

8¼ (8½, 9, 9½, 9¾, 10½, 10½, 11)"
21 (21.5, 23, 24, 25, 26.5, 26.5, 28) cm

13½ (14, 14¾, 15½, 16¾, 18, 18¾, 19¼)"
34.5 (35.5, 37.5, 39.5, 42.5, 45.5, 47.5, 49) cm

17¾ (18, 18, 18¼, 18½, 18½, 18¾, 19)"
45 (45.5, 45.5, 46.5, 47, 47, 47.5, 48.5) cm

BACK & FRONTS

15 (15, 15½, 15½, 16, 16, 16½, 16½)"
38 (38, 39.5, 39.5, 40.5, 40.5, 42, 42) cm

8¾ (8¾, 8¾, 10½, 10½, 10½, 12, 12)"
22 (22, 22, 26.5, 26.5, 26.5, 30.5, 30.5) cm

38 (39, 41, 42¾, 44¼, 47½, 50¼, 54)"
96.5 (99, 104, 108.5, 112.5, 120.5, 127.5, 137) cm

SET-UP ROW: (RS) Sl 1, k1, sm, work Row 1 of *Left Moguls chart* over next 15 sts, pm, (knit to next m, sm) twice, work Row 1 of *Ski Run chart* over next 66 sts, sm, knit to next m, sm, k33 (35, 37, 39, 41, 45, 49, 53), work Row 1 of *Right Moguls chart* over next 15 sts, sm, k2.

NEXT ROW: (WS) Sl 1, p1, sm, work Row 2 of *Right Moguls chart* over next 15 sts, sm, (purl to next m, sm) twice, work Row 2 of *Ski Run chart* over next 66 sts, sm, (purl to next m, sm) twice, work Row 2 of *Left Moguls chart* over next 15 sts, sm, p2.

Cont in established patts until piece measures 15 (15, 15½, 15½, 16, 16, 16½, 16½)" (38 [38, 39.5, 39.5, 40.5, 40.5, 42, 42] cm) from beg, ending with a RS row. Make a note of which row you ended each *Moguls chart* so the pattern can be matched on sleeves.

ARMHOLES

NEXT ROW: (WS) *Work in established patt to 4 (4, 4, 5, 5, 5, 6, 6) sts before side m, BO 8 (8, 8, 10, 10, 10, 12, 12) sts for armhole, removing m; rep from * once more, then work to end of row—186 (192, 202, 206, 214, 230, 240, 258) sts rem; 46 (48, 50, 51, 53, 57, 60, 64) sts for each front, and 94 (96, 102, 104, 108, 116, 120, 130) sts for back.

Set aside.

Sleeves

With dpn, CO 54 (54, 54, 62, 62, 62, 70, 70) sts using the long-tail cast-on method. Pm and join for working in rnds, being careful not to twist sts.

SET-UP RND: [K2, p2] 3 (3, 3, 4, 4, 4, 5, 5) times, pm, k2, p2, k4, [p2, k2] 3 times, p2, k4, p2, k2, pm, [p2, k2] 3 (3, 3, 4, 4, 4, 5, 5) times.

SKI RUN CABLE CHART

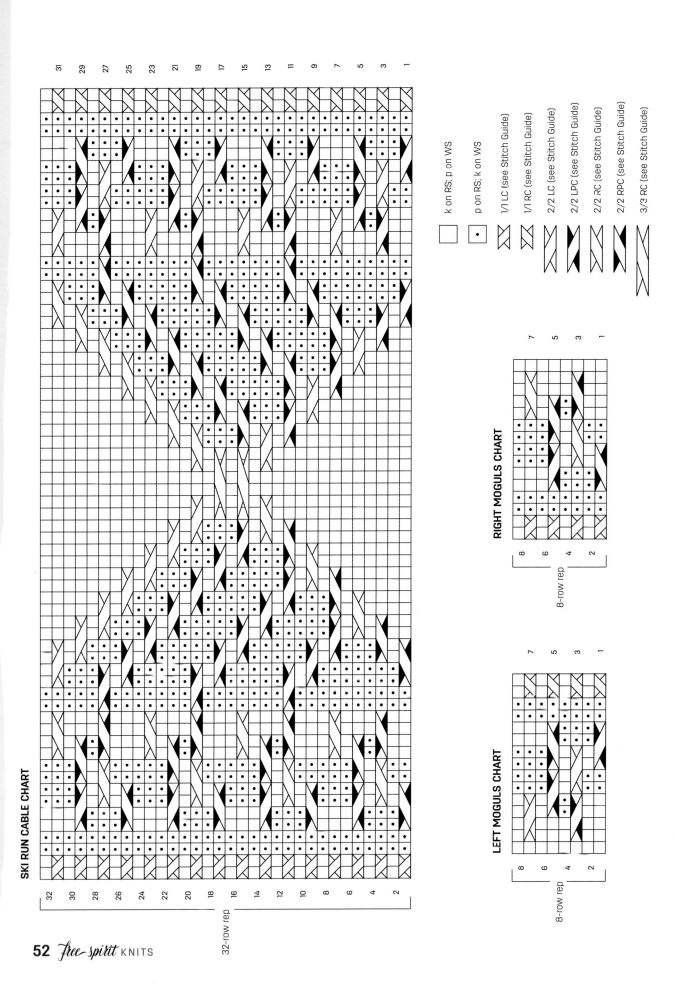

RIGHT MOGULS CHART

LEFT MOGULS CHART

k on RS; p on WS

p on RS; k on WS

1/1 LC (see Stitch Guide)

1/1 RC (see Stitch Guide)

2/2 LC (see Stitch Guide)

2/2 LPC (see Stitch Guide)

2/2 RC (see Stitch Guide)

2/2 RPC (see Stitch Guide)

3/3 RC (see Stitch Guide)

Slipping m as you come to them, work 18 more rnds in established ribbing.

NEXT RND: K12 (12, 12, 16, 16, 16, 20, 20) sts, sm, work Row 1 of *Left Moguls chart* over next 15 sts, and Row 1 of *Right Moguls chart* over next 15 sts, sm, knit to end.

Work 7 (7, 6, 7, 5, 4, 5, 5) rnds even.

INC RND: K1, m1l, work to last st, m1r, k1—2 sts inc'd.

Rep last 8 (8, 7, 8, 6, 5, 6, 6) rnds 11 (12, 14, 12, 15, 18, 16, 17) more times—78 (80, 84, 88, 94, 100, 104, 106) sts.

Cont even until piece measures about 17¾ (18, 18, 18¼, 18½, 18½, 18¾, 19)" (45 [45.5, 45.5, 46.5, 47, 47, 47.5, 48.5] cm) from beg, ending 1 row before the end point on *Moguls Cable charts* as with body, and ending 4 (4, 5, 5, 5, 6, 6) sts before end of last rnd.

BO 8 (8, 8, 10, 10, 10, 12, 12) sts, removing m, then work to end of rnd—70 (72, 76, 78, 84, 90, 92, 94) sts rem.

JOIN BODY AND SLEEVES
With RS facing, cont in established patts, work 46 (48, 50, 51, 53, 57, 60, 64) right front sts, pm, work 70 (72, 76, 78, 84, 90, 92, 94) sleeve sts, pm, work 94 (96, 102, 104, 108, 116, 120, 130) back sts, pm, work 70 (72, 76, 78, 84, 90, 92, 94) sleeve sts, pm, then work 46 (48, 50, 51, 53, 57, 60, 64) left front sts—326 (336, 354, 362, 382, 410, 424, 446) sts.

Work 3 rows even.

SHAPE RAGLAN
Sizes 47½ (50¼, 54)" (120.5 [127.5, 137] cm) only
DOUBLE DEC ROW: (RS) *Work to 2 sts before marker, k3tog, sm, sssk; rep from * 3 more times, work to end of row—16 sts dec'd.

Work 1 WS row even.

Rep last 2 rows 0 (1, 2) more time(s)—394 (392, 398) sts rem; 55 (56, 58) sts for each front, 86 (84, 82) sts for each sleeve, and 112 (112, 118) sts for back.

All sizes

DEC ROW: (RS) *Work to 2 sts before m, k2tog, sm, ssk; rep from * 3 more times, work to end of row—8 sts dec'd.

Work 1 WS row even.

Rep last 2 rows 27 (28, 30, 31, 32, 34, 33, 34) more times—102 (104, 106, 106, 118, 114, 120, 118) sts rem; 18 (19, 19, 19, 20, 20, 22, 23) for each front, 14 (14, 14, 14, 18, 16, 16, 12) for each sleeve, and 38 (38, 40, 40, 42, 42, 44, 48) sts for back.

Hood

NEXT ROW: (RS) Sl 1, k1, work next row of *Left Moguls chart* over next 15 sts, knit to last 17 sts removing m, work next row of *Right Moguls chart* over next 15 sts, k2.

NEXT ROW: (WS) Sl 1, p1, work next row of *Right Moguls chart* over next 15 sts, purl to last 17 sts work next row of *Left Moguls chart* over next 15 sts, p2.

Cont in established patt until hood measures 11 (11, 11, 11, 11, 11¼, 11, 11¼)" (28 [28, 28, 28, 28, 28.5, 28, 28.5] cm) from last row of Ski Run Cable panel at center back, ending with a RS row.

SHAPE HOOD

SET-UP ROW: (WS) Work 51 (52, 53, 53, 59, 57, 60, 59), pm, work 51 (52, 53, 53, 59, 57, 60, 59).

DEC ROW: (RS) Work to 3 sts before marker, k2tog, k1, sm, k1, ssk, work to end—2 sts dec'd.

Work 1 WS row even.

Rep last 2 rows 4 (4, 5, 5, 6, 5, 7, 6) more times, then rep Dec row once more—90 (92, 92, 92, 102, 100, 102, 102) sts rem.

Divide sts evenly with 45 (46, 46, 46, 51, 50, 51, 51) sts on each end of cir needle. Join sts using Kitchener st (see Techniques).

Finishing

Weave in all the loose ends using the ends at the armholes to close up any gaps at the sleeve and body join.

Allow the garment to soak in lukewarm water until thoroughly saturated. Gently press or spin out the excess water. Block the garment to measurements. Allow the garment to dry completely. Sew in the zipper.

Seven Falls, located outside Tuscon, Arizona, is an easily accessible hike that showcases a set of great little waterfalls. Crossing back and forth across Bear Creek Canyon, the trail winds its way across the canyon itself. Accessible year-round, it's a great way to experience some cooling water in the numerous pools while enjoying the canyon's rock formations.

Seven Falls
SCARF

Finished Size
About 75½" (192 cm) long and 4¾" (12 cm) wide.

Yarn
Sport (#2 Fine).

SHOWN HERE: Classic Elite Yarns Fresco (60% wool, 30% alpaca, 10% angora; 164 yd/1¾ oz [50 g]): #5328 Rum Raisin, 3 skeins.

Needles
Size U.S. 6 (4 mm) straight needles.

Adjust needle size if necessary to obtain the correct gauge.

Notions
Cable needle (cn); waste yarn or st holder; tapestry needle.

Gauge
38½ sts and 22 rows = 4" (10 cm) over k2, p2 ribbing.

Notes

The chart is worked back and forth. Read right-side (odd-numbered) rows from right to left and wrong-side (even-numbered) rows from left to right.

STITCH GUIDE

K2, P2 Ribbing *(multiple of 4 sts + 2):*
ROW 1: (RS) *P2, k2; rep from * to last 2 sts, p2.

ROW 2: *K2, k2; rep from * to last 2 sts, k2.

Rep Rows 1 and 2 for patt.

2/2 LC (2 OVER 2 LEFT CROSS): Slip 2 sts to cn and hold in front, k2, k2 from cn.

2/2 LPC (2 OVER 2 LEFT PURL CROSS): Slip 2 sts to cn and hold in front, p2, k2 from cn.

2/2 RPC (2 OVER 2 RIGHT PURL CROSS): Slip 2 sts to cn and hold in back, k2, p2 from cn.

Design Notebook

This scarf is worked in two halves and then grafted in the middle. Cast on at the short end, work the complex cable pattern at the lower end, and then follow with simple ribbing for the remainder of each half.

Scarf
FIRST HALF

CO 46 sts loosely using the long-tail cast-on method (see Techniques).

NEXT ROW: (WS) *K2, p2; rep from * to last 2 sts, k2.

Work 8 more rows as established in k2, p2 ribbing.

Work Rows 1–76 of chart.

Cont in ribbing until piece measures 37¾" (96 cm) from CO edge, or desired length. Cut yarn and place sts on waste yarn or holder.

SECOND HALF

Work the same as for the first half. Cut yarn, leaving a tail about 18" (45.5 cm) long, or 4 times the width of the scarf. Using the Kitchener stitch (see Techniques), graft both halves together.

Finishing

Weave in all the loose ends. Allow the scarf to soak in lukewarm water until thoroughly saturated. Gently press or spin out the excess water. Block the scarf to measurements, patting the cables flat and leaving the ribbing only lightly stretched. Allow the scarf to dry completely.

SEVEN FALLS CHART

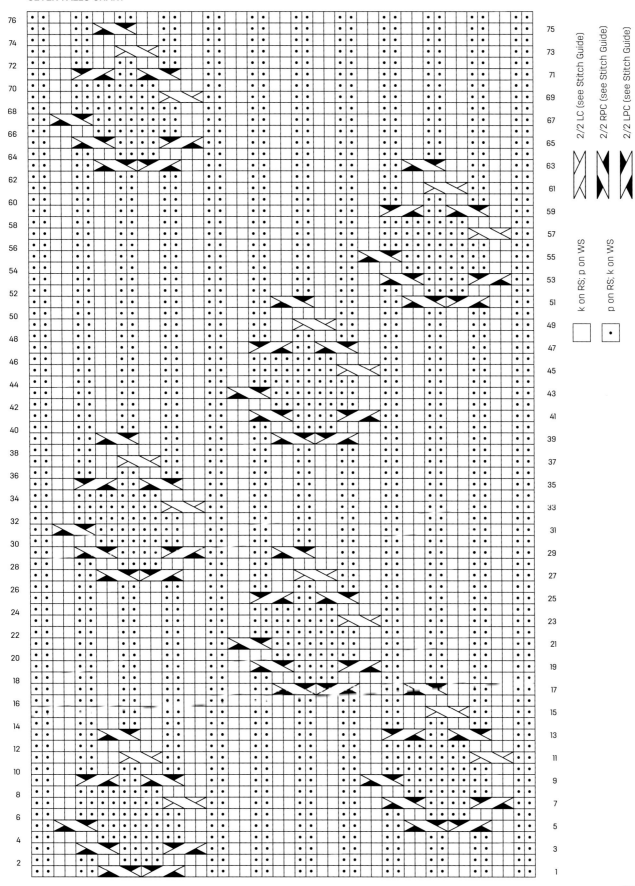

2/2 LC (see Stitch Guide)

2/2 RPC (see Stitch Guide)

2/2 LPC (see Stitch Guide)

k on RS; p on WS

p on RS; k on WS

The yucca, agave, and saguaro plants thrive in some of the most arid conditions in the Southwest United States. They are an important habitat and nutrient resource for the many animals and insects that make their home in this geographic area.

Tres Flores
SHAWL

Finished Size
About 44" (112 cm) wide and 15½" (39.5 cm) long.

Yarn
Fingering weight (#1 Super Fine).

SHOWN HERE: Jamieson and Smith 2-ply Jumper Weight (100% Shetland wool; 125 yd/ [25 g]): #FC62 (light sage green, A), 2 skeins; #141 (medium green, B), 3 skeins; #65 (dark blue-green, C), 4 skeins.

Needles
Size U.S. 5 (3.75 mm) 36" (90 cm) or longer circular (cir).

Adjust needle size if necessary to obtain the correct gauge.

Notions
Stitch markers (m); tapestry needle.

Gauge
23 sts and 31 rows = 4" (10 cm) in Saguaro Flowers chart, after blocking.

Notes

The first 3 and last 3 sts of each row are worked in garter stitch (knit every row) creating a narrow edging on each side. These sts do not appear on the charts.

A circular needle is used to accommodate the large number of stitches after all of the increase rows have been worked.

The charts are worked back and forth. Read the right-side (odd-numbered) rows from right to left and the wrong-side (even-numbered) rows from left to right.

Design Notebook

This semicircular shawl features three distinct lace patterns: A simple textured eyelet representing the flowers of the yucca plant, the wide, overlapping leaves of the agave plant, and a larger floral motif representing the blooms of the saguaro cactus. The increases are incorporated concentrically from the neck to the hem. The shawl is worked beginning at the neck with a garter-stitch tab.

Shawl

With A, CO 3 sts loosely.

Knit 6 rows. Turn piece one-quarter turn to right, pick up and k3 sts in garter st bumps along side of tab, turn piece one-quarter turn to right, pick up and k3 sts along CO edge—9 sts.

SET-UP ROW: (WS) K3, place marker (pm), p3, pm, k3. (The first 3 and last 3 sts of every row are worked in garter st for edging).

INC ROW 1: (RS) K3, sm, [k1f&b] 3 times, sm, k3—12 sts.

Knit 3 rows even.

INC ROW 2: K3, sm, [yo, k1] 6 times, yo, sm, k3—19 sts.

Knit 3 rows even.

INC ROW 3: K3, sm, [yo, k1] 13 times, yo, sm, k3—33 sts.

Knit 3 rows even.

INC ROW 4: K3, sm, [yo, k1] 27 times, sm, k3—60 sts.

Knit 1 row even.

***NEXT ROW:** (RS) K3, work Row 1 of *Yucca Flowers chart* to last 3 sts, k3.

Cont first 3 and last 3 sts in garter st, work Rows 2–20 of chart.*

INC ROW 5: K3, sm, [yo, k1] 54 times, sm, k3—114 sts.

Knit 1 row even.

Rep from * to * once more.

INC ROW 6: K3, sm, [yo, k2tog, yo, k1] 36 times, sm, k3—150 sts.

NEXT (INC) ROW: (WS) Knit to last 4 sts, k1f&b, knit to end of row—151 sts. Cut A.

Join B.

NEXT ROW: (RS) K3, work Row 1 of *Agave Leaf chart* to last 3 sts, k3.

Cont first 3 and last 3 sts in garter st, work Rows 2–42 of chart—223 sts. Cut B.

Join C.

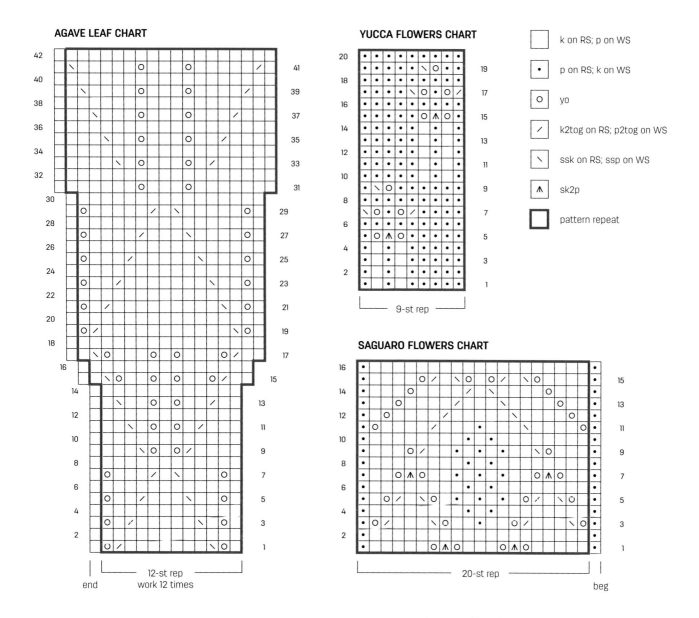

AGAVE LEAF CHART

YUCCA FLOWERS CHART

SAGUARO FLOWERS CHART

12-st rep
work 12 times

end

9-st rep

20-st rep

beg

k on RS; p on WS

• p on RS; k on WS

○ yo

╱ k2tog on RS; p2tog on WS

╲ ssk on RS; ssp on WS

Λ sk2p

pattern repeat

INC ROW 7: K3, sm, [k1, yo] 24 times, [k1, yo, k2tog, yo] 56 times, [k1, yo] 24 times, k1, sm, k3—327 sts.

Knit 1 row even.

*NEXT ROW: (RS) K3, work Row 1 of *Saguaro Flowers chart* to last 3 sts, k3.

Cont first 3 and last 3 sts in garter st, work Rows 2–16 of chart.

Knit 2 rows even.

NEXT ROW: (RS) K3, sm, [k2tog, yo] to last 4 sts, k1, sm, k3.*

Knit 1 row even.

Rep from * to * once more.

Knit 3 rows even.

BO all sts loosely kwise.

Finishing

Weave in all the loose ends, leaving long ends to trim after blocking. Allow the shawl to soak in lukewarm water until thoroughly saturated. Gently press or spin out the excess water. Block the shawl to measurements, pulling out each point along the BO edge. Allow the shawl to dry completely. Trim the loose ends.

Mesa Verde (Spanish for green table) is the largest archaeological site in the United States. Mesa Verde National Park was created in 1906 by Theodore Roosevelt to preserve the numerous cliff dwellings and village ruins of the indigenous Ancient Pueblo people. The cliff dwellings in the park are built within natural cave and cliff outcroppings, and their natural-colored rock and adobe structures blend almost seamlessly into the cliffs, topped by the green sage-covered flat mesa above them.

Mesa Verde
SHAWL

Finished Size
About 38½" (98 cm) at widest point with ends curved and 14" (35.5 cm) long.

Yarn
Fingering weight (#1 Super Fine).

SHOWN HERE: The Fibre Company Canopy Fingering (50% baby alpaca, 30% merino, 20% viscose bamboo; 200 yd/1 ¾ oz [50 g]): Wild Ginger (MC), 1 skein; Conifer (CC), 1 skein.

Needles
Size U.S. 7 (4.5 mm) 24" (60 cm) long circular (cir) needle.

Adjust needle size if necessary to obtain the correct gauge.

Notions
Tapestry needle.

Gauge
18 sts and 35½ rows = 4" (10 cm) over patt after blocking.

Notes

It is very important to work the slipped stitches along the edges LOOSELY in this pattern. The slipped stitches help create a soft curved upper edge and give the shawl its unique shape. Pulling too firmly on these stitches will not allow the shawl to block easily, so err on the side of too loose versus too tight. When slipping the edge stitches on wrong side (even-numbered) rows, always slip the stitch with the yarn held in the front.

When slipping stitches for the textured striped sections, always slip the stitch with the yarn held in front (on the right side of the work).

You may choose to LOOSELY strand the unused color along the right-hand edge. If you do that, be sure to twist the yarns every other row to catch the loose strand of the unused yarn along the edge.

Design Notebook

This boomerang-shaped shawl begins with a short cast-on edge. It is shaped with increases on every row along one side, and decreases on every other row along the opposite side, creating an elongated triangular shape. It features stockinette and slip-stitch textured stripes along its length.

Shawl

With MC, CO 9 sts loosely using the long-tail cast-on method (see Techniques).

NEXT ROW: (WS) Purl.

ROW 1: (RS) K1f&b, knit to last 2 sts, k2tog.

ROW 2: Sl 1 wyf, purl to last 2 sts, p1f&b, sl 1 wyf—1 st inc'd.

ROWS 3–6: Rep Rows 1 and 2 twice—2 sts inc'd.

ROWS 7 AND 8: With CC, rep Rows 1 and 2—1 st inc'd.

ROWS 9–16: Rep Rows 1–8—4 sts inc'd.

ROWS 17 AND 18: With MC, rep Rows 1 and 2—1 st inc'd.

ROWS 19 AND 20: With CC, rep Rows 7 and 8—1 st inc'd.

ROW 21: With MC, k1f&b, knit to last 2 sts, k2tog.

ROW 22: Sl 1 wyf, knit to last 2 sts, p1f&b, sl 1 wyf—1 st inc'd.

ROW 23: With CC, k1f&b, (sl 1 wyf, k1) to last 3 sts, sl 1 wyf, k2tog.

ROW 24: Sl 1 wyf, knit to last 2 sts, p1f&b, sl 1 wyf—1 st inc'd.

ROWS 25 AND 26: With MC, rep Rows 23 and 24—1 st inc'd.

ROW 27: K1f&b, knit to last 2 sts, k2tog.

ROW 28: Sl 1 wyf, purl to last 2 sts, p1f&b, sl 1 wyf—1 st inc'd.

ROWS 29 AND 30: With CC, rep Rows 23 and 24—1 st inc'd.

ROWS 31 AND 32: With CC, rep Rows 21 and 22—1 st inc'd.

ROWS 33 AND 34: With MC, rep Rows 25 and 26—1 st inc'd.

ROWS 35 AND 36: With CC, rep Rows 23 and 24—1 st inc'd.

ROWS 37 AND 38: With CC, rep Rows 27 and 28—1 st inc'd.

ROWS 39 AND 40: With MC, rep Rows 23 and 24—1 st inc'd.

ROWS 41–231: Rep Rows 1–40 four more times, then rep Rows 1–31 once more   124 sts. Cut MC.

BO all sts loosely pwise.

Finishing

Weave in all the loose ends, leaving long ends to trim after blocking. Allow the shawl to soak in lukewarm water until thoroughly saturated. Gently press or spin out the excess water. Block the shawl to measurements, shaping top (inc) edge into a graceful curve, and the remaining edges straight. Allow the shawl to dry completely. Trim the loose ends.

The saguaro cactus is native to Arizona and its tall, tree-like shapes are easily spotted against the bright blue spring skies in the Sonoran Desert. In the spring, the cactus plants produce large, creamy white flower blossoms. These pretty flowers are pollinated primarily by bats that are attracted by the night-blooming blossoms with their very sweet nectar.

Saguaro Blossom HAT

Finished Size
About 18" (45.5 cm) brim circumference and 7¾" (19.5 cm) tall.

Yarn
Worsted weight (#4 Medium).

SHOWN HERE: The Fibre Company Organik (70% organic wool, 15% alpaca, 15% silk; 98 yd/1¾ oz [50 g]): Fjord, 2 skeins.

Needles
Size U.S. 7 (4.5 mm) 16" (40 cm) circular (cir) and set of 4 or 5 double-pointed needles (dpn).

Adjust needle size if necessary to obtain the correct gauge.

Notions
Stitch marker (m); cable needle (cn); tapestry needle.

Gauge
26½ sts and 33 rnds = 4" (10 cm) in chart patt after blocking.

Note

This hat is worked in the round from the pattern chart. Read all rows from right to left.

STITCH GUIDE

2/2 LC (2 OVER 2 LEFT CROSS): Slip 2 sts to cn and hold in front, k2, k2 from cn.

2/2 LPC (2 OVER 2 LEFT PURL CROSS): Slip 2 sts to cn and hold in front, p2, k2 from cn.

2/2 RC (2 OVER 2 RIGHT CROSS): Slip 2 sts to cn and hold in back, k2, k2 from cn.

2/2 RPC (2 OVER 2 RIGHT PURL CROSS): Slip 2 sts to cn and hold in back, k2, p2 from cn.

K1-tbl, P1 Ribbing *(even number of sts)*
All rnds: *K1-tbl, p1; rep from *.

Design Notebook

This tam-shaped hat is cast on at the ribbing and worked upward with shaping increases for the crown. The crown is decorated with a cable pattern reminiscent of a saguaro blossom, with decreases shaping the crown worked between the cabled motifs.

SAGUARO BLOSSOM CHART

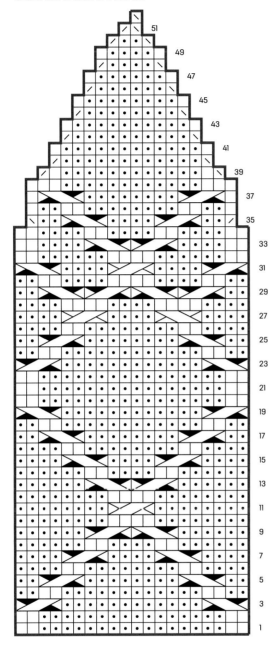

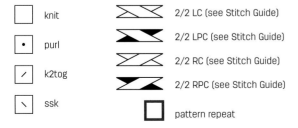

	knit
	purl
	k2tog
	ssk

	2/2 LC (see Stitch Guide)
	2/2 LPC (see Stitch Guide)
	2/2 RC (see Stitch Guide)
	2/2 RPC (see Stitch Guide)
	pattern repeat

Hat

With cir needle, CO 94 sts loosely using the long-tail cast-on method (see Techniques). Place marker (pm) and join for working in rnds, being careful not to twist sts.

Work 12 rnds in K1-tbl, P1 Ribbing.

NEXT (INC) RND: *K2, m1; rep from * to last 2 sts, k2—140 sts.

Work Rnds 1–52 of chart patt, changing to dpn when there are too few sts to comfortably work on cir needle—7 sts rem.

Knit 4 rnds even. Cut yarn, leaving a 12" (30.5 cm) tail and thread tail through rem sts. Pull tightly to close hole and fasten off on WS.

Finishing

Weave in all the loose ends. Allow the hat to soak in lukewarm water until thoroughly saturated. Gently press or spin out the excess water. Insert a 10" (25.5 cm) diameter cardboard blocker or dinner plate into the hat, patting the cables flat on the top and leaving the ribbing for the band unstretched. Allow the hat to dry completely.

The San Juan Mountains span the border between northeastern New Mexico and southeastern Colorado. Now filled with ghost towns and visited by off-road Jeep tours and skiers, these high, rugged peaks were home to numerous silver mines in the late 1800s. The mountain range runs north to south and on clear winter days here in northern New Mexico, I can see the peaks extending north of the Colorado border from my back deck. Glints of snow cover the dark gray rocks.

San Juans
SWEATER

Finished Size
About 45¼ (46¾, 48½, 52½, 54¼, 56, 60¾, 67¼)" (115 (118.5, 123, 133.5, 138, 142, 154.5, 171) cm chest circumference, and 25¼ (26, 26, 26¼, 26¼, 26½, 26¾, 26¾)" (64 [66, 66, 66.5, 66.5, 67.5, 68, 68] cm) long.

Project shown measures 54¼" (138 cm).

Yarn
DK weight (#3 Light).

SHOWN HERE: Berroco Ultra Alpaca Light (50% alpaca, 50% wool; 144 yd/1 ¾ oz [50 g]): #4209 Moonshadow (light gray, A), 9 (9, 9, 10, 10, 11, 12, 13) skeins; #4207 Salt and Pepper (dark gray, B), 3 (3, 3, 4, 4, 5, 6, 7) skeins; #4201 Winter White (C), 3 (3, 3, 4, 4, 5, 6, 7) skeins.

Needles
Main body and sleeves: Size U.S. 5 (3.75 mm) 24" (60 cm) or longer circular (cir) or straight for the body.

FRONT BANDS AND NECKBAND: Size U.S. 5 (3.75 mm) 40" (100 cm) or longer circular (cir).

THREE-NEEDLE BIND-OFF: Two size U.S. 5 (3.75 mm) double-pointed (dpn).

Adjust needle size if necessary to obtain the correct gauge.

Notions
Stitch markers (m); stitch holders or waste yarn; tapestry needle; nine ¾" (19 mm) buttons; sewing needle; sewing thread.

Gauge
19½ sts and 44 rows = 4" (10 cm) in Mountain Peaks chart, after blocking; 25 sts and 34 rows = 4" (10 cm) in K4, P4 Ribbing lightly stretched, after blocking.

The chart is worked back and forth. Read the right-side (odd-numbered) rows from right to left and the wrong-side (even-numbered) rows from left to right.

Circular needles are used to accommodate the large number of stitches. Do not join.

STITCH GUIDE

K4, P4 Ribbing *(multiple of 8 sts):*

ROW 1: (RS) *K4, p4; rep from *.

ROW 2: (WS) *P4, k4; rep from *.

Rep Rows 1 and 2 for patt.

Back

With shorter cir or straight needles and A, CO 110 (118, 126, 130, 138, 146, 154, 170) sts using the long-tail cast-on method (see Techniques).

NEXT ROW: (WS) K1, place marker (pm), [p4, k4] to last 5 (5, 5, 1, 1, 1, 1, 1) st(s), p4 (4, 4, 0, 0, 0, 0, 0), pm, k1.

NEXT ROW: (RS) P1, sm, k4 (4, 4, 0, 0, 0, 0, 0), [p4, k4] to last st, sm, p1.

Cont in established ribbing until piece measures 3" (7.5 cm), ending with a WS row.

NEXT ROW: (RS) K2tog, working Row 1 of **Mountain Peaks chart**, work st at right

end of chart, 4-st rep to last 3 sts, work 2 sts at left end of chart, k1—109 (117, 125, 129, 137, 145, 153, 169) sts.

Cont first and last st of every row in St st (knit on RS, purl on WS), work Rows 2–12 of chart, then rep Rows 1–12 until piece measures 17¼ (17½, 17, 17¼, 16¾, 16¾, 16¾, 16¼)" (44 [44.5, 43, 44, 42.5, 42.5, 42.5, 41.5] cm) from beg, ending with a WS row.

SHAPE ARMHOLES

BO 4 (5, 5, 5, 6, 6, 7, 8) sts at beg of next 2 rows—101 (107, 115, 119, 125, 133, 139, 153) sts rem.

Work even until armholes measure 8 (8½, 9, 9, 9½, 9¾, 10, 10½)" (20.5 [21.5, 23, 23, 24, 25, 25.5, 26.5] cm], ending with a WS row.

Design Notebook

The sweater is a unisex cardigan-style jacket with a ribbed shawl collar, cuffs, and hem. It has a boxy fit with modified dropped shoulders and an overall textured slip-stitch pattern in shades of gray and off-white. The sweater is knit in pieces from the bottom up to the shoulders. The sleeves are knit separately and then sewn in. The sweater is finished with a shawl collar of k4, p4 ribbing to match the hems.

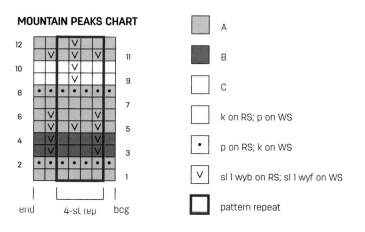

MOUNTAIN PEAKS CHART

| A |
| B |
| C |

k on RS; p on WS

• p on RS; k on WS

V sl 1 wyb on RS; sl 1 wyf on WS

pattern repeat

end   4-st rep   beg

With RS facing, place first 29 (30, 32, 32, 33, 34, 37, 43) sts on holder or waste yarn for right shoulder, center 43 (47, 51, 55, 59, 65, 65, 67) sts on holder or waste yarn for back neck, and rem 29 (30, 32, 32, 33, 34, 37, 43) sts on holder or waste yarn for left shoulder.

Right Front

With shorter cir or straight needles and A, CO 52 (52, 52, 60, 60, 60, 68, 76) sts using the long-tail cast-on method (see Techniques).

NEXT ROW: (WS) K1, pm, [p4, k4] to last 3 sts, p2, pm, k1.

NEXT ROW: (RS) P1, sm, k2, [p4, k4] to last st, sm, p1.

Cont in established ribbing until piece measures 3" (7.5 cm), ending with a WS row.

NEXT ROW: (RS) Working Row 1 of the **Mountain Peaks chart**, work st at right end of the chart, 4-st rep to last 3 sts, work 2 sts at the left end of the chart, k1.

Work Rows 2–12 of chart, then rep Rows 1–12 until piece measures 17¼ (17½, 17, 17¼, 16¾, 16¾, 16¾, 16¼)" (44 [44.5, 43, 44, 42.5, 42.5, 42.5, 41.5] cm) from beg, ending with a RS row.

SHAPE ARMHOLE AND NECK

NEXT ROW: (WS) BO 4 (5, 5, 5, 6, 6, 7, 8) sts, work in established patt to end—48 (47, 47, 55, 54, 54, 61, 68) sts rem.

NECK DEC ROW: (RS) Work next row of chart, k1, ssk, work in patt to end—1 st dec'd.

Rep Neck Dec row every 4 rows 18 (16, 14, 22, 20, 19, 23, 24) more times—29 (30, 32, 32, 33, 34, 37, 43) sts rem.

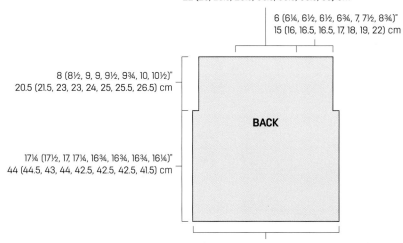

8¾ (9¾, 10½, 11¼, 12, 13¼, 13¼, 13¾)"
22 (25, 26.5, 28.5, 30.5, 33.5, 33.5, 35) cm

6 (6¼, 6½, 6½, 6¾, 7, 7½, 8¾)"
15 (16, 16.5, 16.5, 17, 18, 19, 22) cm

8 (8½, 9, 9, 9½, 9¾, 10, 10½)"
20.5 (21.5, 23, 23, 24, 25, 25.5, 26.5) cm

BACK

17¼ (17½, 17, 17¼, 16¾, 16¾, 16¾, 16¼)"
44 (44.5, 43, 44, 42.5, 42.5, 42.5, 41.5) cm

22¼ (24, 25¾, 26½, 28, 29¾, 31½, 34¾)"
56.5 (61, 65.5, 67.5, 71, 75.5, 80, 88.5) cm

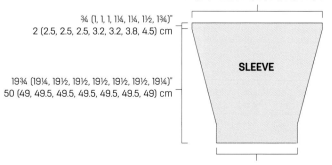

21¼ (21¼, 22¼, 22¼, 24, 24½, 24¾, 26½)"
54 (54, 56.5, 56.5, 61, 62, 63, 67.5) cm

¾ (1, 1, 1, 1¼, 1¼, 1½, 1¾)"
2 (2.5, 2.5, 2.5, 3.2, 3.2, 3.8, 4.5) cm

SLEEVE

19¾ (19¼, 19½, 19½, 19½, 19½, 19½, 19¼)"
50 (49, 49.5, 49.5, 49.5, 49.5, 49.5, 49) cm

13¼ (13¼, 13¼, 13¼, 13¼, 13¼, 14¾, 14¾)"
33.5 (33.5, 33.5, 33.5, 33.5, 33.5, 37.5, 37.5) cm

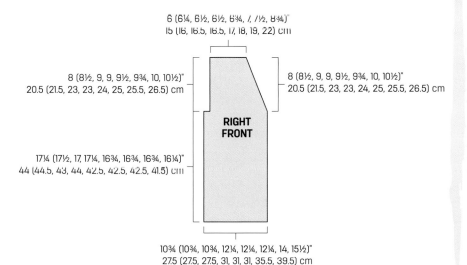

6 (6¼, 6½, 6½, 6¾, 7, 7½, 8¾)"
15 (16, 16.5, 16.5, 17, 18, 19, 22) cm

8 (8½, 9, 9, 9½, 9¾, 10, 10½)"
20.5 (21.5, 23, 23, 24, 25, 25.5, 26.5) cm

8 (8½, 9, 9, 9½, 9¾, 10, 10½)"
20.5 (21.5, 23, 23, 24, 25, 25.5, 26.5) cm

RIGHT FRONT

17¼ (17½, 17, 17¼, 16¾, 16¾, 16¾, 16¼)"
44 (44.5, 43, 44, 42.5, 42.5, 42.5, 41.5) cm

10¾ (10¾, 10¾, 12¼, 12¼, 12¼, 14, 15½)"
27.5 (27.5, 27.5, 31, 31, 31, 35.5, 39.5) cm

Work even until the armhole measures 8 (8½, 9, 9, 9½, 9¾, 10, 10½)" (20.5 [21.5, 23, 23, 24, 25, 25.5, 26.5] cm), ending with a WS row. Place rem sts on holder or waste yarn.

Left Front

Work same as right front until piece measures 17¼ (17½, 17, 17¼, 16¾, 16¾, 16¾, 16¼)" (44 [44.5, 43, 44, 42.5, 42.5, 42.5, 41.5] cm) from beg, ending with a WS row.

SHAPE ARMHOLE AND NECK

NEXT ROW: (RS) BO 4 (5, 5, 5, 6, 6, 7, 8) sts, work to end—48 (47, 47, 55, 54, 54, 61, 68) sts rem.

Work 1 WS row even.

NECK DEC ROW: (RS) Work in established patt to last 3 sts, k2tog, k1—1 st dec'd. Rep neck dec row every 4 rows 18 (16, 14, 22, 20, 19, 23, 24) more times—29 (30, 32, 32, 33, 34, 37, 43) sts rem.

Work even until armhole measures 8 (8½, 9, 9, 9½, 9¾, 10, 10½)" (20.5 [21.5, 23, 23, 24, 25, 25.5, 26.5] cm), ending with a WS row. Place rem sts on holder or waste yarn.

Sleeves

With shorter cir or straight needles and A, CO 64 (64, 64, 64, 64, 64, 72, 72) sts loosely using the long-tail cast-on method.

NEXT ROW: (WS) K2, pm, [p4, k4] to last 6 sts, p4, pm, k2.

NEXT ROW: (RS) P2, sm, [k4, p4] to last 6 sts, k4, sm, p2.

Cont in established ribbing until piece measures 3" (7.5 cm), ending with a WS row.

NEXT (INC) ROW: (WS) Work in established ribbing to last 6 sts, p1f&b, k3, sm, p2—65 (65, 65, 65, 65, 65, 73, 73) sts.

NEXT ROW: (RS) K1, working Row 1 of **Mountain Peaks chart**, work st at right end of chart, 4-st rep to last 3 sts, work 2 sts at left end of chart, k1.

Cont first and last st of every row in St st, work 3 rows even in established patt.

INC ROW: (RS) K1, m1r, work in established patt to last st, m1l, k1—2 sts inc'd.

Rep Inc row every 6 rows 0 (0, 6, 6, 20, 22, 12, 27) times, every 8 rows 9 (9, 15, 15, 5, 4, 11, 0) times, then every 10 rows 9 (9, 0, 0, 0, 0, 0, 0) times—103 (103, 109, 109, 117, 119, 121, 129) sts. Work new sts into patt.

Cont even until piece measures 20 (20¼, 20½, 20½, 20¾, 20¾, 21, 21)" (51 [51.5, 52, 52, 52.5, 52.5, 53.5, 53.5] cm) from beg, ending with a WS row. BO all sts kwise with A.

Finishing

Weave in all the loose ends. Join the shoulders using the three-needle bind-off (see Techniques).

Buttonband

With longer cir needle and A, with RS facing, beg at lower right front edge, pick up and k93 (95, 92, 94, 94, 93, 92, 89) sts along right front edge to beg of neck shaping, 40 (44, 45, 45, 47, 49, 50, 52) sts along right front neck, knit held 21 (23, 25, 27, 29, 32, 32, 33) back neck sts, k2tog, knit rem held 20 (22, 24, 26, 28, 31, 31, 32) back neck sts, pick up and k40 (44, 45, 45, 47, 49, 50, 52) sts along left front neck, pm, then 93 (95, 92, 94, 94, 93, 92, 89) sts along left front edge to lower edge—308 (324, 324, 332, 340, 348, 348, 348) sts.

NEXT ROW: (WS) P4, [k4, p4] to end.

Cont in established ribbing until band measures 1½" (3.8 cm), ending with a WS row.

BUTTONHOLE ROW: (RS) Work in established ribbing to 4 (4, 4, 5, 5, 4, 4, 6) sts past m, *BO 3 sts in patt for buttonhole, work in patt until there are 7 (7, 7, 7, 7, 7, 7, 6) sts after BO gap; rep from * 7 more times, BO 3 sts in patt, work to end.

NEXT ROW: (WS) *Work in ribbing to buttonhole gap, CO 3 sts using the backward-loop method (see Techniques); rep from * 8 more times, work to end.

Work 6 more rows in established ribbing. BO all sts loosely in patt.

Sew in sleeves. Sew side and underarm seams.

Allow the garment to soak in lukewarm water until thoroughly saturated. Gently press or spin out the excess water. Block the garment to measurements, being careful not to stretch the ribbing too much. Don't allow it to pull in significantly; you may find it helpful to pin the hems so they dry flat. Allow the garment to dry completely.

Sew buttons to the right band opposite the buttonholes.

Toltec Gorge is a deep canyon that runs north and south through the mountains of northern New Mexico. The gorge has railroad tracks running through it for use by the Cumbres & Toltec Scenic Railroad, a historic train built in 1880 to connect the silver mining towns in the San Juan Mountains. The train takes visitors through the mountains and along the edge of the rocky gorge daily to view the gorgeous scenery of the region.

Toltec Gorge
COWL

Finished Size
About 18" (45.5 cm) circumference and 5¾" (14.5 cm) tall.

Yarn
DK weight (#3 Light)

SHOWN HERE: Malabrigo Silky Merino (51% silk, 49% merino wool, 150 yd [137 m]/1¾ oz [50 g]): #66 Lavanda (MC); #435 Turquoise (CC), 1 skein each color.

Needles
Size U.S. 5 (3.75 mm) 16" (40 cm) circular (cir).

Adjust needle size if necessary to obtain the correct gauge.

Notions
Markers (m); tapestry needle.

Gauge
24½ sts and 32 rnds = 4" (10 cm) in chart patt after blocking.

Notes

The cowl is worked in the round following the chart. Read all rounds from right to left.

Design Notebook

This is a great beginner stranded-knitting piece. This cowl is worked in the round using DK weight yarn and easy two-color stranded-knitting pattern. The piece is cast on at the bottom hem and then worked upward following the chart. The colorwork pattern is a stylized version of train tracks running through the Toltec Gorge in the Rockies of northern New Mexico into Colorado.

Cowl

With MC, CO 110 sts loosely using the long-tail cast-on method (see Techniques). Place marker (pm) and join for working in rnds, being careful not to twist sts.

(Purl 1 rnd, knit 1 rnd) twice.

Work Rnds 1–38 of chart. Cut CC.

(Knit 1 rnd, purl 1 rnd) twice. BO all sts loosely kwise.

Finishing

Weave in all the loose ends. Soak the cowl in lukewarm water until thoroughly saturated. Gently press or spin out the excess water. Lay the cowl flat, patting into shape, but do not overly stretch the fabric. Allow the cowl to dry completely.

☐ MC

☒ CC

☐ pattern repeat

TOLTEC GORGE CHART

(chart: 5-st rep, work 22 times; rounds numbered 1–37, odd numbers shown)

5-st rep
work 22 times

Santa Fe is New Mexico's capital city. It has an eclectic mix of architecture that features neutral-colored adobe walls, but many homes and stores throughout the city have wooden doors painted brilliant turquoise blue or purple.

Santa Fe
WRAP

Finished Size
About 63" (160 cm) long x 24" (61 cm) wide.

Yarn
DK weight (#3 Light).

SHOWN HERE: Wooly Wonka Fibers Nimue DK (50% silk, 50% merino wool; 230 yd/3½ oz [100 g]): Spice (A), 4 skeins; Terracotta (B), 1 skein; Turquoise (C), 1 skein; Raven's Wings (D), 2 skeins; Heartsease (E), 1 skein.

Needles
Size U.S. 8 (5 mm) straight or 24" (60 cm) or longer circular (cir) needle.

Adjust needle size if necessary to obtain the correct gauge.

Notions
Stitch markers (m); waste yarn or spare needle; tapestry needle.

Gauge
19½ sts and 29 rows = 4" (10 cm) over St stitch; 19½ sts and 35 rows = 4" (10 cm) over chart.

Notes

Three stitches at each edge are worked in garter stitch to form a narrow border. These stitches are not shown on the chart.

When working the charted slipped-stitch sections, be sure to carry the working yarn loosely to prevent puckering. When slipping stitches on right-side rows, slip each stitch purlwise with the yarn in back, and when slipping stitches on wrong-side rows, slip each stitch purlwise with the yarn in front.

Right-side (odd-numbered) rows on the chart are read from right to left, and wrong-side (even-numbered) rows are read from left to right.

When working the narrow stockinette stripes and the chart, carry the unused color loosely up the side of the work and twist the yarns when changing colors to catch the loose strand at the edge.

STITCH GUIDE

Garter Stitch
Knit all sts every row.

Stockinette Stitch
ROW 1: (RS) Knit.

ROW 2: (WS) Purl.

Rep Rows 1 and 2 for pattern.

Design Notebook

This rectangular shawl is knit from one short end to the center. The second half is then knit, and the two pieces are grafted together at the center. A simple slip-stitch pattern highlights each end of the wrap. The remainder of the piece is knit in stockinette, with narrow stripes of bright colors as accents.

Shawl

FIRST HALF

With A, CO 118 sts loosely using the long-tail cast-on method (see Techniques).

NEXT ROW: (WS) K3, place marker (pm), knit to last 3 sts, pm, k3.

Knit 2 more rows, slipping m when you come to them.

NEXT ROW: (RS) Keeping first 3 sts and last 3 sts in garter st, work 24 rows in St st, ending with a WS row. Cut A.

Stripe Pattern

*With B, work 8 rows in St st with garter st edges. Cut B. With D, work 4 rows in St st with garter st edges.

SANTA FE CHART

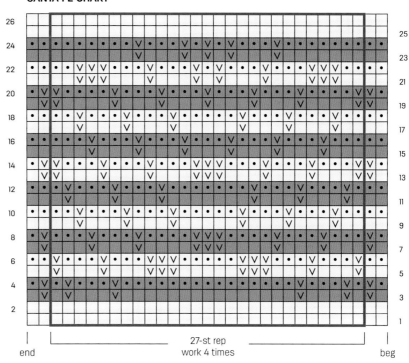

27-st rep
work 4 times

end   beg

	C
	D
	k on RS, p on WS
•	p on RS; k on WS
V	sl 1 wyb on RS; sl 1 wyf on WS
	pattern repeat

Do not cut D. With E, work 2 rows in St st with garter st edges. Cut E. With D, work 4 rows in St st with garter st edges. Cut D. With B, work 8 rows in St st with garter st edges. Cut B.*

With A, work 24 rows in St st with garter st edges. Cut A.

NEXT ROW: (RS) With C, k3, work Row 1 of chart to last 3 sts, k3.

Work Rows 2–26 of chart as established. Cut C and D.

With A work 8 rows in St st with garter st edges. Cut A.

Work chart Rows 1–26 again.

With A, work 24 rows in St st with garter st edges.

Rep Stripe patt from * to * once more.

With A, work 48 rows in St st with garter st edges. Cut A. Place sts on waste yarn or spare needle. Piece measures about 31½" (80 cm) long.

SECOND HALF

Work same as for the first half. Cut A, leaving a tail about 96" (244 cm) long, or 4 times longer than the width of the shawl.

Using Kitchener st (see Techniques), graft both halves together.

Finishing

Weave in all the loose ends, leaving the ends long until after blocking. Allow the shawl to soak in lukewarm water until thoroughly saturated. Gently press or spin out the excess water. Block the shawl to measurements. Allow the shawl to dry completely. Trim all the loose ends.

The Churro sheep are extremely important to the Navajo people. These hardy, compact animals are able to graze on the scrubby vegetation and survive the arid conditions in the high desert. They are utilized not only for a food source, but they also provide fiber for clothing, rugs, and blankets. Navajo weavers use the gorgeous natural colors of their sheep to create geometric designs with a striking, timeless quality. I was fortunate enough to spend an afternoon with a mother/daughter team who raise Churros, to learn more about the breed and process the wool on traditional Navajo supported spindles.

Churro Sheep
COWL

Finished Size
About 42¾" (108.5 cm) circumference and 9¾" (25 cm) tall.

Yarn
Fingering (#1 Super Fine)

SHOWN HERE: Elemental Affects Natural Shetland Fingering (100% North American Shetland wool, 118 yd/1 oz [28.35g]): Musket (light gray, A), 2 skeins; Emsket (dark gray, B), 2 skeins; Fawn (light brown, C), 2 skeins; Moorit (dark brown, D), 1 skein.

Needles
Size U.S. 3 (3.25 mm) 32" (80 cm) circular (cir).

Adjust needle size if necessary to obtain the correct gauge.

Notions
Markers (m); tapestry needle.

Gauge
25½ sts and 37 rnds = 4" (10 cm) in chart pattern after blocking.

Design Notebook

This long, drapable cowl is knitted in the round using natural sheep wool colors. The cowl features bands of stylized sheep and geometric motifs inspired by woven Navajo rugs. Due to the limited shaping and finishing, this cowl would be a great starter project for the knitter who wants to learn stranded knitting with traditional Shetland jumper-weight yarns.

Cowl

With C, CO 273 sts loosely using long-tail method (see Techniques). Place marker (pm) and join for working in rnds, being careful not to twist sts.

(Purl 1 rnd, knit 1 rnd) twice.

Work Rnds 1–79 of chart patt.

With C, (knit 1 rnd, purl 1 rnd) twice. BO all sts loosely kwise.

Finishing

Weave in all the loose ends. Thoroughly soak the cowl in lukewarm water. Gently press or spin out the excess water. Lay the cowl flat, patting into shape, but do not overly stretch the fabric. Allow the cowl to dry completely.

□	A	⊙	D
●	B	□	pattern repeat
✕	C		

CHURRO SHEEP CHART

79
77
75
73
71
69
67
65
63
61
59
57
55
53
51
49
47
45
43
41
39
37
35
33
31
29
27
25
23
21
19
17
15
13
11
9
7
5
3
1

13-st rep
work 21 times

For a brief time in the late winter and early spring, the desert of Arizona comes to life with bright floral blooms. Saguaro cactus blossoms, bottlebrush, and weeping dalea flowers provide a brilliant contrast to the muted greens of the sagebrush and cacti. This cheerful show is short-lived, however, and the desert landscape quickly returns to its more neutral palette of sand and pale green as the summer begins.

Arizona Spring
SWEATER

Finished Size

About 29¾ (31½, 33¼, 35½, 37¾, 40½, 43¾, 48¼)" (75.5 [80, 84.5, 90, 96, 103, 111, 122.5] cm) bust circumference, and 19½ (20, 20, 20¾, 21½, 22, 22¾, 23¼)" (49.5 [51, 51, 52.5, 54.5, 56, 58, 59] cm long.

Project shown measures 31½" (80 cm).

Yarn

Fingering weight (#1 Super Fine).

SHOWN HERE: Jamieson and Smith's 2-ply Jumper Weight (100% Shetland wool; 125 yd [25 g]): #FC24 (sage green, A), 6 (7, 8, 9, 10, 11, 12, 13) balls; #43 (dark pink, B), 1 (1, 1, 2, 2, 2, 3, 3) ball(s); #FC22 (medium pink, C), 1 (1, 1, 2, 2, 2, 3, 3) ball(s); #FC50 (pale pink, D), 1 (1, 1, 2, 2, 2, 3, 3) ball(s); #28 (yellow, E), 1 (1, 1, 1, 2, 2, 2, 2) balls.

Needles

BODY: Size U.S. 2 (2.75 mm) 24" (60 cm) or longer circular (cir).

SLEEVES AND NECKLINE: Size U.S. 2 (2.75 mm) double-pointed (dpn).

Notions

Stitch markers (m); waste yarn or stitch holders; tapestry needle.

Gauge

29 sts and 37 rnds = 4" (10 cm) in Corrugated Ribbing, after blocking;

26 sts and 42 rnds = 4" (10 cm) in St st, after blocking;

28 sts and 44 rnds = 4" (10 cm) in Cactus Flower chart patt, after blocking.

STITCH GUIDE

Corrugated Ribbing (multiple of 3 sts)

RNDS 1–7: *K2 with A, p1 with B; rep from *.

RNDS 8–14: *K2 with A, p1 with C; rep from*.

RNDS 15–21: *K2 with A, p1 with D; rep from *.

K2, P1 Ribbing (multiple of 3 sts)
All rnds: *K2, p1; rep from *.

Design Notebook

This women's short-sleeve sweater is knit in the round from the hem up. It features corrugated ribbing at the hem. It is shaped with waist and bust darts for a trim fit. The yoke of the sweater is worked with two simple stranded-colorwork floral patterns. It requires only minimal finishing to complete.

Body

With cir needle and A, CO 237 (252, 264, 279, 294, 321, 348, 378) sts using long-tail cast-on method (see Techniques). Place marker (pm) and join for working in rnds, being careful not to twist sts.

NEXT RND: *K2, p1; rep from *.

Work Rnds 1–21 of Corrugated Ribbing.

Cont with A only, beg St st (knit every rnd).

NEXT (DEC) RND: Knit and dec 3 (0, 0, 1, 0, 1, 0, 0) st(s) evenly spaced—234 (252, 264, 278, 294, 320, 348, 378) sts.

SET-UP RND: K39 (42, 44, 46, 49, 53, 58, 63), pm for left front dart, k39 (42, 44, 47, 49, 54, 58, 63), pm for right front dart, k39 (42, 44, 46, 49, 53, 58, 63), pm for right side, k39 (42, 44, 46, 49, 53, 58, 63), pm for right back dart, k39 (42, 44, 47, 49, 54, 58, 63), pm for left back dart, k39 (42, 44, 46, 49, 53, 58, 63).

Work 3 rnds even.

SHAPE WAIST

NEXT (DEC) RND: *Work to 3 sts before dart m, k2tog, k1, sm, k1, ssk; rep from *—8 sts dec'd.

Rep dec rnd every 4 rnds 6 (7, 7, 7, 7, 8, 8, 9) more times—178 (188, 200, 214, 230, 248, 276, 298) sts rem.

Work 8 (8, 8, 16, 16, 16, 32, 16) rnds even.

SHAPE BUST

NEXT (INC) RND: * Work to 1 st before dart m, m1r, k1, sm, k1, m1l; rep from *—8 sts inc'd.

Rep Inc rnd every 15 rnds 1 (1, 1, 1, 1, 1, 0, 1) more time(s)—194 (204, 216, 230, 246, 264, 284, 314) sts. Remove dart m after last inc rnd; retain side and beg-of-rnd m.

Work even until piece measures 12½ (13, 13, 13½, 13½, 14, 14½, 15)" (31.5 [33, 33, 34.5, 34.5, 35.5, 37, 38] cm), ending last rnd 7 (7, 8, 8, 10, 9, 8, 10) sts before end of rnd.

Armholes

BO 15 (14, 16, 16, 20, 18, 16, 20) sts, work to 7 (7, 8, 8, 10, 9, 8, 10) sts before next m, BO 15 (14, 16, 16, 20, 18, 16, 20) sts, work to end—164 (176, 184, 198, 206, 228, 252, 274) sts rem; 82 (88, 92, 99, 103, 114, 126, 137) each for front and back. Set aside.

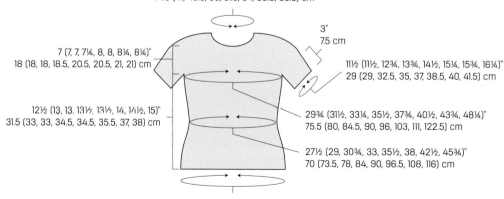

17½ (18½, 19½, 19¾, 20¼, 21¼, 23, 25)"
44.5 (47, 49.5, 50, 51.5, 54, 58.5, 63.5) cm

3"
7.5 cm

7 (7, 7, 7¼, 8, 8, 8¼, 8¼)"
18 (18, 18, 18.5, 20.5, 20.5, 21, 21) cm

11½ (11½, 12¾, 13¾, 14½, 15¼, 15¾, 16¼)"
29 (29, 32.5, 35, 37, 38.5, 40, 41.5) cm

12½ (13, 13, 13½, 13½, 14, 14½, 15)"
31.5 (33, 33, 34.5, 34.5, 35.5, 37, 38) cm

29¾ (31½, 33¼, 35½, 37¾, 40½, 43¾, 48¼)"
75.5 (80, 84.5, 90, 96, 103, 111, 122.5) cm

27½ (29, 30¾, 33, 35½, 38, 42½, 45¾)"
70 (73.5, 78, 84, 90, 96.5, 108, 116) cm

32¾ (34¾, 36½, 38½, 40½, 44¼, 48, 52¼)"
83 (88.5, 92.5, 98, 103, 112.5, 122, 132.5) cm

Sleeves

With dpn and A, CO 84 (84, 93, 99, 105, 111, 114, 117) sts using the long-tail cast-on method. Pm and join for working in rnds, being careful not to twist sts.

NEXT RND: *K2, p1; rep from *.

Work Rnds 1–21 of Corrugated Ribbing.

Cont with A only, beg St st. Work 4 rnds, end last rnd 7 (7, 8, 8, 9, 9, 9, 10) sts before end of rnd.

BO 14 (14, 16, 16, 18, 18, 18, 20) sts, then knit to end—70 (70, 77, 83, 87, 93, 96, 97) sts rem.

JOIN BODY AND SLEEVES

With cir needle, k70 (70, 77, 83, 87, 93, 96, 97) sts for left sleeve, pm, work 82 (88, 92, 99, 103, 114, 126, 137) sts for front, pm, k70 (70, 77, 83, 87, 93, 96, 97) sts for right sleeve, pm, k82 (88, 92, 99, 103, 114, 126, 137) sts for back—304 (316, 338, 364, 380, 414, 444, 468) sts. Pm and join for working in rnds.

NEXT (DEC) RND: Knit and dec 0 (4, 2, 4, 4, 6, 4, 4) sts evenly spaced, placing dec at each side of sleeves if possible—304 (312, 336, 360, 376, 408, 440, 464) sts rem.

Work 4 (4, 4, 6, 6, 6, 6, 6) rnds even, removing all but beg-of-rnd m on last rnd.

Work rnds 1–7 of **Desert Blooms chart.**

With A only, knit 3 rnds.

Yoke
YOKE DEC RND 1

SIZE 29¾"(75.5 cm): K5, k2tog, *k2, k2tog; rep from * 72 more times, work to end—230 sts rem.

CACTUS FLOWER CHART

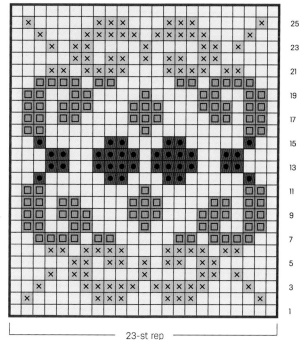

23-st rep

DESERT BLOOMS CHART

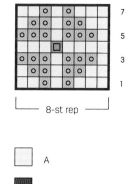

8-st rep

A	
B	
C	
D	
E	
pattern repeat	

SIZE 31½" (80 cm): [K4, k2tog] twice, *[k3, k2tog] 3 times, k4, k2tog; rep from * 13 more times, k4, k2tog—253 sts rem.

SIZE 33¼" (84.5 cm): K5, k2tog, *k3, k2tog, k4, k2tog; rep from * 28 more times, k3, k2tog, work to end—276 sts rem.

SIZE 35½" (90 cm): [K4, k2tog] 5 times, *k3, k2tog, [k4, k2tog] 7 times; rep from * 6 more times, work to end—299 sts rem.

SIZE 37¾" (96 cm): K2, k2tog, *k5, k2tog; rep from * 52 more times, work to end—322 sts rem.

SIZE 40½" (103 cm): K3, k2tog, *k4, k2tog, k5, k2tog; rep from * 30 more times—345 sts rem.

SIZE 43¾" (111 cm): K6, k2tog, *k4, k2tog; rep from * 70 more times, work to end—368 sts rem.

SIZE 48¼" (122.5 cm): K2tog, *k5, k2tog, [k4, k2tog] twice; rep from * 23 more times, work to end—391 sts rem.

Work 2 (2, 2, 2, 4, 4, 4, 4) rounds even in St st.

Work rnds 1–26 of **Cactus Flower chart.**

With A only, knit 1 (1, 1, 2, 2, 2, 2) rnd(s).

YOKE DEC RND 2

SIZE 29¾" (75.5 cm): K2, k2tog, *k3, k2tog; rep from * 44 more times, work to end—184 sts rem.

SIZE 31½" (80 cm): K2, k2tog, *k2, k2tog, [k3, k2tog] 3 times; rep from * 12 more times, work to end—200 sts rem.

SIZE 33¼" (84.5 cm): K2, *k3, k2tog, k2, k2tog; rep from * 29 more times, work to end—216 sts rem.

SIZE 35½" (90 cm): K2tog, *k2, k2tog, k3, k2tog; rep from * 32 more times—232 sts rem.

SIZE 37¾" (96 cm): *[K3, k2tog] 4 times, k2, k2tog; rep from * 12 more times, k3, k2tog, knit to end—256 sts rem.

SIZE 40½" (103 cm): K2tog, *[k3, k2tog] 3 times, k2, k2tog; rep from * 17 more times, work to end—272 sts rem.

SIZE 43¾" (111 cm): K6, k2tog, *k3, k2tog; rep from * 70 more times, work to end—296 sts rem.

SIZE 48¼" (122.5 cm): K4, k2tog, *k3, k2tog, k4, k2tog; rep from * 34 more times—320 sts rem.

Work 2 (2, 2, 2, 4, 4, 4, 4) rounds even in St st.

Work rnds 1–7 of **Desert Blooms chart.**

With A only, knit 2 rnds.

YOKE DEC RND 3

SIZE 29¾" (75.5 cm): *K1, [k1, k2tog, k2tog] 5 times; rep from * 6 more times, work to end—114 sts rem.

SIZE 31½" (80 cm): *K1, [k2tog] twice; rep from *—120 sts rem.

SIZE 33¼" (84.5 cm): K3, *k1, [k2tog] 3 times; rep from * 29 more times, work to end—126 sts rem.

SIZE 35½" (90 cm): *K1, [k2tog] 4 times; rep from * 24 more times, k1, [k2tog] 3 times—129 sts rem.

SIZE 37¾" (96 cm): [K2tog] 4 times, *k1, [k2tog] 15 times; rep from *—132 sts rem.

SIZE 40½" (103 cm): [K2tog] twice, *k1, [k2tog] 33 times; rep from *—138 sts rem.

SIZES 43¾ AND 48¼" (111 [122.5] cm): K2, [k2tog] to last 2 sts, work to end—150 (162) sts rem.

Knit 1 (1, 1, 2, 2, 2, 2) rnd(s) even.

Neckband

Work 6 (6, 6, 6, 8, 8, 10, 10) rnds in K2, P1 Ribbing. BO all sts loosely in patt.

Finishing

Weave in all the loose ends. Sew the underarm seams. Allow the garment to soak in lukewarm water until thoroughly saturated. Gently press or spin out the excess water. Block the garment to measurements, pinning hems so they dry flat. Allow the garment to dry completely.

Central Arizona's Salt River area has one of the few remaining wild horse herds in the United States. This group of animals forages along the banks of the river, and while the precise location of the herd remains a closely kept secret to prevent them from being disturbed, members of the herd can often be seen grazing along the edges of the Mesa River by kayakers.

Salt River SWEATER

Finished Size
About 30 (33½, 36½, 40, 43, 46, 49½)" (76 [85, 92.5, 101.5, 109, 117, 125.5] cm) chest circumference, and 25¼ (25½, 26½, 27, 27½, 28¼, 29)" (64 [65, 67.5, 68.5, 70, 72, 73.5] cm) long.

Project shown measures 43" (109 cm).

Yarn
Worsted weight (#4 Medium).

SHOWN HERE: Harrisville Highland (100% virgin wool; 200 yd/3½ oz [100 g]): #56 Jude, 6 (6, 7, 7, 8, 8, 9) skeins.

Needles
BODY: Size U.S. 5 (3.75 mm) 24" (60 cm) or longer circular (cir).

COLLAR: Size U.S. 5 (3.75 mm) set of 5 double-pointed (dpn).

SLEEVES: Size U.S. 5 (3.75 mm) 24" (60 cm) circular (cir) or straight.

Adjust needle size if necessary to obtain the correct gauge.

Notions
Stitch markers (m); cable needle (cn); stitch holders or waste yarn; tapestry needle.

Gauge
20 sts and 31 rows = 4" (10 cm) in Double seed st, after blocking; 76-st Salt River chart = 13¾" (35 cm) wide; 35-st Salt River Sleeve chart = 5¼" (13.5 cm) wide, after blocking.

Notes

The charts are worked back and forth. Read all right-side (odd-numbered) rows from right to left and all wrong-side (even-numbered) rows from left to right.

A circular needle is used to knit the front and back pieces to accommodate the large number of stitches. Work back and forth; do not join.

Design Notebook

This men's/unisex pullover is knitted in pieces from the bottom up, with modified dropped shoulders. The sleeves are knitted from the cuff up. The pieces are sewn together and a ribbed neckband is added. The center cable motif represents the Salt River and is flanked by small horseshoe cables and twisted-stitch marsh grass motifs. Double seed-stitch panels finish the sides and the undersides of the sleeves.

STITCH GUIDE

Double seed stitch *(multiple of 4 sts)*

ROW 1: (RS) *K2, p2; rep from *.

ROWS 2 AND 4: (WS) Knit the knit sts and purl the purl sts.

ROW 3: *P2, k2; rep from *.

Rep Rows 1–4 for patt.

K2, P2 Ribbing *(multiple of 4 sts)*

ROW 1: (RS) *K2, p2; rep from *.

ROW 2: (WS) Knit the knit sts and purl the purl sts.

Rep Rows 1–2 for patt.

1/1 LT (1 OVER 1 LEFT TWIST): Sl 1 st to cn and hold in front, k1, k1 from cn.

1/1 LPT (1 OVER 1 LEFT PURL TWIST): Sl 1 st to cn and hold in front, p1, k1 from cn.

1/1 RT (1 OVER 1 RIGHT TWIST): Sl 1 st to cn and hold in back, k1, k1 from cn.

1/1 RPT (1 OVER 1 RIGHT PURL TWIST): Sl 1 st to cn and hold in back, k1, p1 from cn.

1/2 LC (1 OVER 2 LEFT CROSS): Sl 1 st to cn and hold in front, k2, k1 from cn.

1/2 RC (1 OVER 2 RIGHT CROSS): Sl 2 sts to cn and hold in back, k1, k2 from cn.

2/1 LPC (2 OVER 1 LEFT PURL CROSS): Sl 2 sts to cn and hold in front, p1, k2 from cn.

2/1 RPC (2 OVER 1 RIGHT PURL CROSS): Sl 1 st to cn and hold in back, k2, p1 from cn.

2/2 LC (2 OVER 2 LEFT CROSS): Sl 2 sts to cn and hold in front, k2, k2 from cn.

2/2 RC (2 OVER 2 RIGHT CROSS): Sl 2 sts to cn and hold in back, k2, k2 from cn.

Back

With cir needle, CO 84 (92, 100, 108, 116, 124, 132) sts loosely using the long-tail cast-on method (see Techniques). Do not join.

SET-UP ROW: (WS) [P2, k2] 1 (2, 3, 4, 5, 6, 7) time(s), place marker (pm), [k3, p3] twice, k3, p1 tbl, k1, p2, k2, p2, k1, p1 tbl, [k2, p4] 4 times, k2, p1 tbl, k1, p2, k2, p2, k1, p1 tbl, [k3, p3] twice, k3, pm, [k2, p2] 1 (2, 3, 4, 5, 6, 7) time(s).

NEXT ROW: (RS) [K2, p2] 1 (2, 3, 4, 5, 6, 7) time(s), sm, [p3, k3] twice, p3, k1 tbl, p1, k2, p2, k2, p1, k1 tbl, [p2, k4] 4 times, p2, k1 tbl, p1, k2, p2, k2, p1, k1 tbl, [p3, k3] twice, p3, sm, [p2, k2] 1 (2, 3, 4, 5, 6, 7) time(s).

Cont in established ribbing until piece measures 2½" (6.5 cm), ending with a WS row.

NEXT ROW: (RS) Work Row 1 of Double seed st over first 4 (8, 12, 16, 20, 24, 28) sts, sm, work Row 1 of **Salt River chart** to next m, sm, work Row 1 of Double seed st to end.

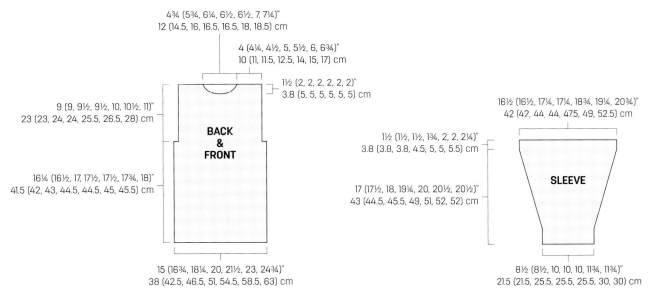

4¾ (5¾, 6¼, 6½, 6½, 7, 7¼)"
12 (14.5, 16, 16.5, 16.5, 18, 18.5) cm

4 (4¼, 4½, 5, 5½, 6, 6¾)"
10 (11, 11.5, 12.5, 14, 15, 17) cm

1½ (2, 2, 2, 2, 2, 2)"
3.8 (5, 5, 5, 5, 5, 5) cm

9 (9, 9½, 9½, 10, 10½, 11)"
23 (23, 24, 24, 25.5, 26.5, 28) cm

BACK & FRONT

16¼ (16½, 17, 17½, 17½, 17¾, 18)"
41.5 (42, 43, 44.5, 44.5, 45, 45.5) cm

15 (16¾, 18¼, 20, 21½, 23, 24¾)"
38 (42.5, 46.5, 51, 54.5, 58.5, 63) cm

16½ (16½, 17¼, 17¼, 18¾, 19¼, 20¾)"
42 (42, 44, 44, 47.5, 49, 52.5) cm

1½ (1½, 1½, 1¾, 2, 2, 2¼)"
3.8 (3.8, 3.8, 4.5, 5, 5, 5.5) cm

SLEEVE

17 (17½, 18, 19¼, 20, 20½, 20½)"
43 (44.5, 45.5, 49, 51, 52, 52) cm

8½ (8½, 10, 10, 10, 11¾, 11¾)"
21.5 (21.5, 25.5, 25.5, 25.5, 30, 30) cm

k on RS; p on WS

p on RS; k on WS

k1 tbl on RS; p1 tbl on WS

1/1 RT (see Stitch Guide)

1/1 LT (see Stitch Guide)

1/1 RPT (see Stitch Guide)

1/1 LPT (see Stitch Guide)

2/1 RPC (see Stitch Guide)

2/1 LPC (see Stitch Guide)

1/2 RC (see Stitch Guide)

1/2 LC (see Stitch Guide)

2/2 RC (see Stitch Guide)

2/2 LC (see Stitch Guide)

pattern repeat

SALT RIVER CHART

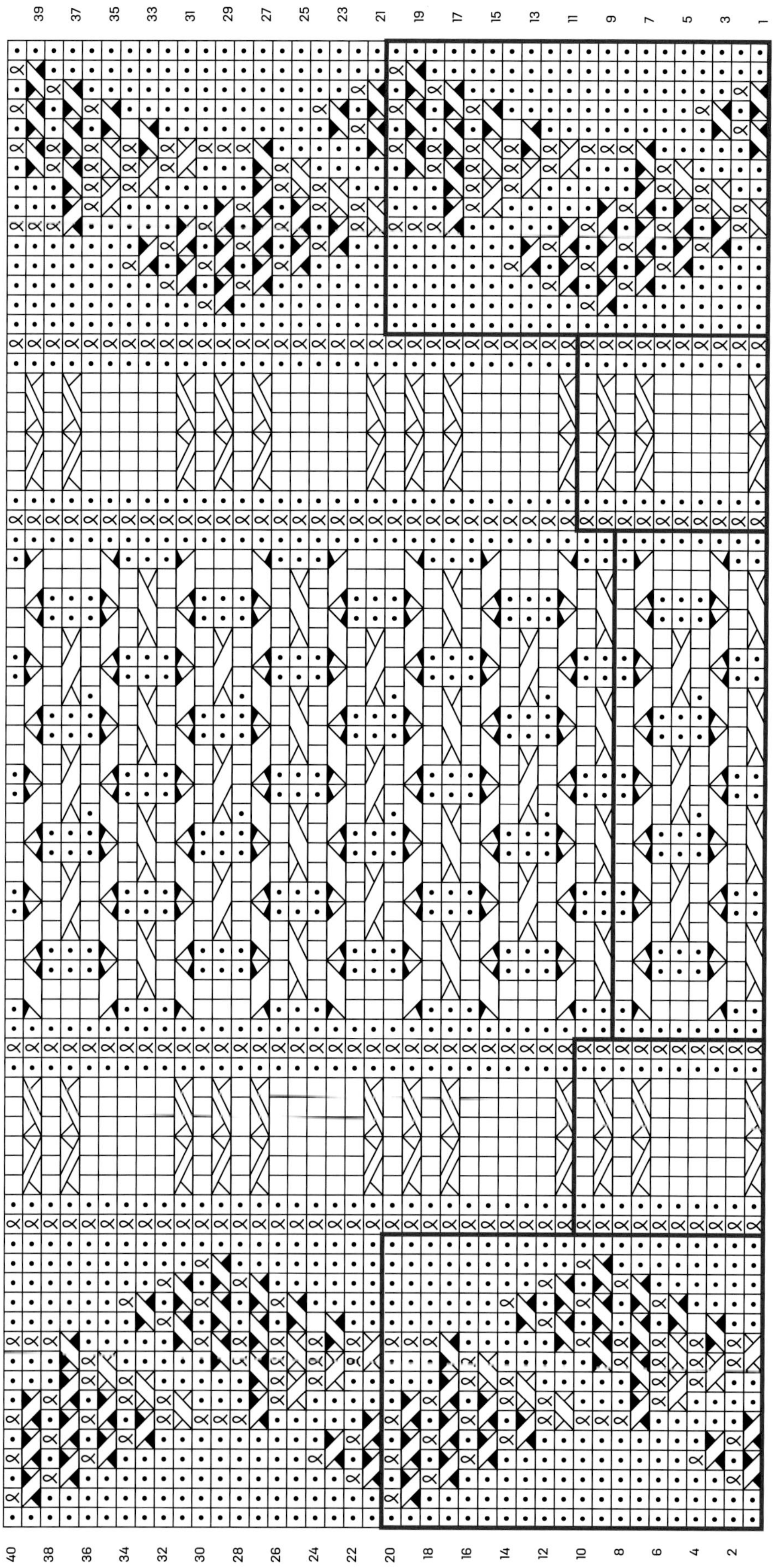

SALT RIVER SLEEVE CHART

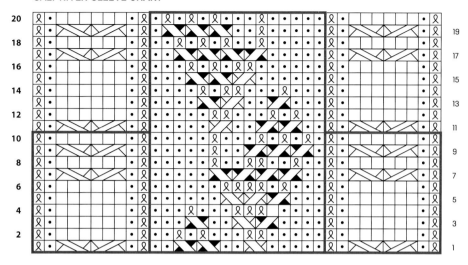

Cont in established patts until piece measures 16¼ (16½, 17, 17½, 17½, 17¾, 18)" (41.5 [42, 43, 44.5, 44.5, 45, 45.5] cm) from beg, ending with a WS row.

Note: Each section of the chart has a different number of rows to their repeat. The charts show multiples of each section until all sections end with a complete repeat.

Armholes

BO 7 (7, 8, 9, 10, 10, 11) sts at beg of next 2 rows—70 (78, 84, 90, 96, 104, 110) sts rem.

Cont in established patt until armholes measure 9 (9, 9½, 9½, 10, 10½, 11)" (23 [23, 24, 24, 25.5, 26.5, 28] cm), ending with a WS row.

Note: For size 30" (76 cm), the panels at each side of the body will not be worked in their entirety. Work left and right twists when there are enough sts to do so; when there are not enough sts

to work a twist, work those sts either knitwise or purlwise according to the pattern.

NEXT ROW: (RS) BO 22 (23, 25, 27, 30, 33, 35) sts, cont in patt until 26 (32, 34, 36, 36, 38, 40) sts have been worked since last BO st, then BO rem 22 (23, 25, 27, 30, 33, 35) sts. Place rem 26 (32, 34, 36, 36, 38, 40) sts on holder for neck.

Front

Work as for back until armholes measure 7½ (7, 7½, 7½, 8, 8½, 9)" (19 [18, 19, 19, 20.5, 21.5, 23] cm), ending with a WS row.

SHAPE NECK

NEXT ROW: (RS) Work 28 (32, 34, 37, 39, 42, 44) sts in established patt, place center 14 (14, 16, 16, 18, 20, 22) sts on holder or waste yarn for neck, join a second ball of yarn and work to end— 28 (32, 34, 37, 39, 42, 44) sts rem each side. Work both sides at same time with separate balls of yarn. BO 3 sts at each neck edge once, then 1 st 3 (6, 6, 7, 6, 6, 6) times—22 (23, 25, 27, 30, 33, 35) sts rem each side. Cont in established patt until armholes measure 9 (9, 9½, 9½, 10, 10½, 11)" (23 [23, 24, 24, 25.5, 26.5, 28] cm), ending with a RS row.

BO all sts in patt.

Sleeves

With cir or straight needles, CO 51 (51, 59, 59, 59, 67, 67) sts loosely using the long-tail cast-on method.

SET-UP ROW: (WS) [P2, k2] 2 (2, 3, 3, 3, 4, 4) times, pm, p1 tbl, k1, p2, k2, p2, k1, p1 tbl, [k3, p3] twice, k3, p1 tbl, k1, p2, k2, p2, k1, p1 tbl, pm, [k2, p2] 2 (2, 3, 3, 3, 4, 4) times.

NEXT ROW: (RS) [K2, p2] 2 (2, 3, 3, 3, 4, 4) times, sm, k1 tbl, p1, k2, p2, k2, p1, k1 tbl, [p3, k3] twice, p3, k1 tbl, p1, k2, p2, k2, p1, k1 tbl, sm, [p2, k2] 2 (2, 3, 3, 3, 4, 4) times.

Cont in established ribbing until the piece measures 2½" (6.5 cm), ending with a WS row.

NEXT ROW: (RS) Work Row 1 of Double seed st over first 8 (8, 12, 12, 12, 16, 16) sts, sm, work Row 1 of **Salt River Sleeve chart** to next m, sm, work Row 1 of Double seed st to end.

Work 1 WS row in established patt.

INC ROW: (RS) K1, m1l, work in established patt to last st, m1r, k1—2 sts inc'd.

Rep Inc row every 4 rows 8 (5, 0, 0, 0, 0, 0) times, every 6 rows 11 (14, 12, 8, 18, 9, 21) times, then every 8 rows 0 (0, 5, 9, 2, 9, 0) times—91 (91, 95, 95, 101, 105, 111) sts. Work new sts into Double seed st.

Cont even until piece measures 18½ (19, 19½, 21, 22, 22½, 22¾)" (47 [48.5, 49.5, 53.5, 56, 57, 58] cm), ending with a WS row.

BO all sts kwise.

Finishing

Weave in all the loose ends. Sew the shoulder seams, matching cables and twisted sts.

Neckband

With dpn and RS facing, beg at right shoulder seam, knit held 26 (32, 34, 36, 36, 38, 40) back neck sts, pick up and k22 (23, 23, 24, 25, 27, 27) sts along left front neck, knit held 14 (14, 16, 16, 18, 20, 22) front neck sts, then pick up and k22 (23, 23, 24, 25, 27, 27) sts along right front neck—84 (92, 96, 100, 104, 112, 116) sts. Pm and join for working in rnds.

NEXT RND: *K2, p2; rep from *.

Work 19 more rnds in established ribbing. BO all sts loosely in patt.

Sew the side seams. Sew the BO edge of sleeves to the vertical edges of the armholes, centering charted patt at the shoulder seam. Sew the BO edges of the armholes to the sides of the sleeves. Sew the underarm seams.

Allow the garment to soak in luke-warm water until thoroughly saturated. Gently press or spin out the excess water. Block to measurements, allowing the ribbing to remain unblocked to retain stretchiness. Allow the garment to dry completely.

Chaco Canyon was an area of flourishing building and culture for the Pueblo peoples between A.D. 900 and 1150. The area contains one of the densest concentrations of Pueblo building complexes in the Southwest. Many Chacoan buildings may have been aligned to capture the solar and lunar cycles, and there is some proposed belief that the buildings functioned as a large solar observatory. The area was abandoned following a fifty-year period of drought, and it is now preserved as a park/historical site in the arid and sparsely populated Four Corners area.

Chaco Canyon

SHAWL

Finished Size
About 49½" (125.5 cm) wide and 18¼" (46.5 cm) long.

Yarn
Fingering weight (#1 Super Fine).

SHOWN HERE: Sweet Georgia Yarns Silk Crush (50% superwash merino wool, 50% silk; 375 yd [343 m]/ 4 oz [115 g]): Cayenne (MC), 1 skein; Nightshade (CC), 2 skeins.

Needles
Size U.S. 4 (3.5 mm): 32" (80 cm) or longer circular (cir).

Adjust needle size if necessary to obtain the correct gauge.

Notions
Stitch markers (m); 980 size 6/0 seed beads; size U.S. 14 (0.75 mm) crochet hook; tapestry needle

Gauge
22 sts and 37 rows = 4" (10 cm) in St st.

Notes

The first three and last three stitches of every row are knit, creating a garter-stitch border along the front edges.

When working from the charts, work right-side (odd-numbered) rows from right to left and wrong-side (even-numbered) rows from left to right.

Beads are added using the crochet-hook method. To place beads, knit or purl the next stitch in the pattern, place a bead onto the crochet hook, insert the hook into the stitch just worked and pull stitch through bead, place the stitch back onto right-hand needle tip, gently snugging the bead to lay flat.

Design Notebook

This shawl is constructed from the neck down in a half-hexagon/semicircular shape. Increases are worked along four rays from the center back neck, and the body of the shawl is worked in stockinette stripes, incorporating these increases. The bottom border features a wide panel of beaded motifs representing various constellations and star patterns.

Shawl

With cir needle and MC, CO 3 sts.

Knit 6 rows. Turn piece one-quarter turn to right, pick up and k3 sts in garter st bumps along side of tab, turn piece one-quarter turn to right, pick up and k3 sts along CO edge—9 sts.

SET-UP ROW: (WS) K3, pm, p3, pm, k3.

INC ROW 1: (RS) K3, sm, (k1f&b) 3 times, sm, k3—12 sts.

INC ROW 2: (WS) K3, sm, p1, p1f&b, p2, p1f&b, p1, sm, k3—14 sts.

INC ROW 3: (RS) K3, sm, k1f&b, k1, pm, k1f&b, k2, k1f&b, pm, k1, k1f&b, sm, k3—18 sts.

NEXT ROW AND ALL OTHER WS ROWS TO BOTTOM BORDER: K3, purl to last 3 sts, slipping m as you come to them, k3.

INC ROW 4: (RS) K3, sm, k1f&b, knit to m, sm, k1f&b, [knit to 1 st before m, k1f&b, sm] twice, k3—4 sts inc'd.

Rep last 2 rows 21 more times, ending with a WS row—106 sts; 3 sts on each side of border, 25 sts in each side section, and 50 sts in center section.

STRIPES

Rep Inc row 4 every RS row and at the same time, work stripes as foll: [2 rows CC, 4 rows MC] 7 times, [4 rows CC, 2 rows MC] 7 times—274 sts; 3 sts on each side of border, 67 sts in each side section, and 134 sts in center section.

CHART A

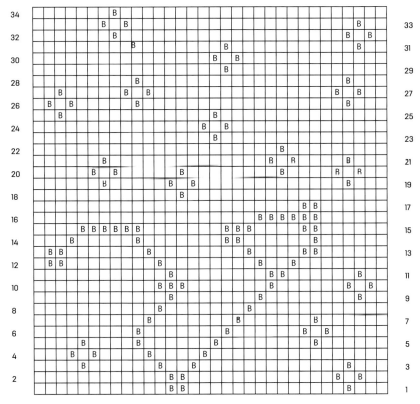

32 sts

Note: When changing colors, carry the unused color loosely up the side edge of the work.

Remove center 2 m on last row, leaving m at each edge. Cut MC.

BOTTOM BORDER

SET-UP ROW: (RS) With CC, k3, sm, k32, pm, [k40, pm, k11, pm] twice, k32, [pm, k11, pm, k40] twice, sm, k3.

NEXT ROW: K3, purl to last 3 sts, slipping m as you come to them, k3.

NEXT ROW: (RS) K3, sm. Working Row 1 of each chart, work chart A over next 32 sts, sm, work chart B over next 40 sts, sm, **Stars chart** over next 11 sts, sm, chart C over next 40 sts, sm,

CHART B

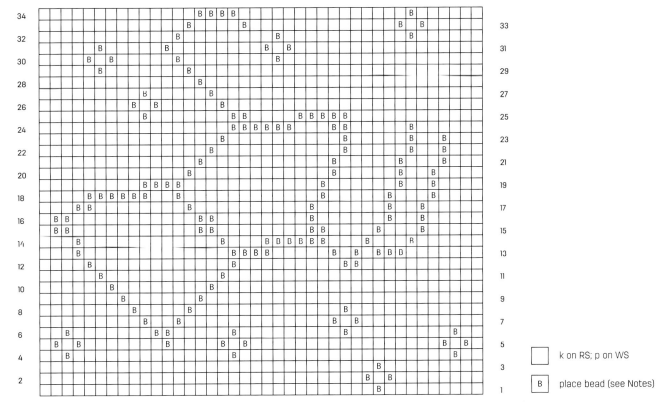

40 sts

□ k on RS; p on WS

B place bead (see Notes)

CHART C

k on RS; p on WS

B place bead (see Notes)

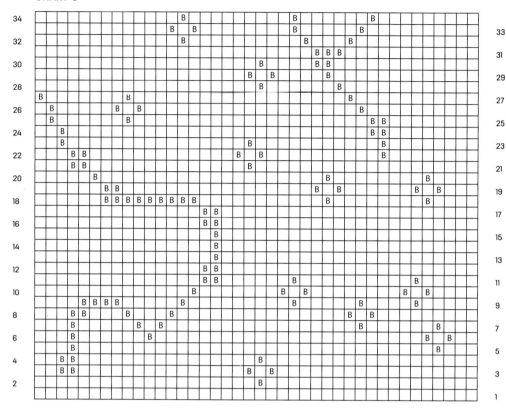

40 sts

STARS CHART

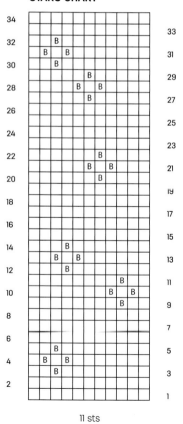

11 sts

CHART D

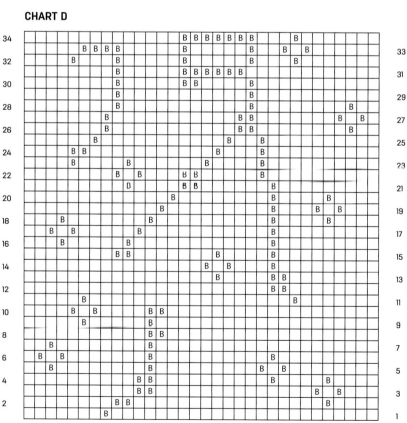

32 sts

CHART E

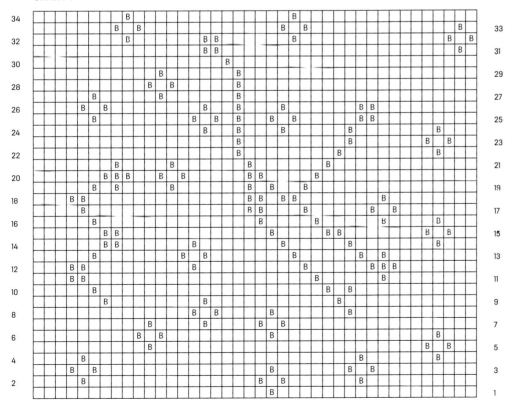

40 sts

CHART F

40 sts

Stars chart over next 11 sts, sm, chart D over next 32 sts, sm, **Stars chart** over next 11 sts, sm, chart E over next 40 sts, sm, **Stars chart** over next 11 sts, sm, chart F over next 40 sts, sm, k3.

NEXT ROW: K3, sm, working Row 2 of each chart, work chart F over next 40 sts, sm, work **Stars chart** over next 11 sts, sm, chart E over next 40 sts, sm, work **Stars chart** over next 11 sts, sm, work chart D over next 32 sts, sm, work **Stars chart** over next 11 sts, sm, work chart C over next 40 sts, sm, work

Stars chart over next 11 sts, sm, work chart B over next 40 sts, sm, work chart A over next 32 sts, sm, k3.

Work Rows 3–34 of charts as established.

Knit 5 rows. BO all sts loosely kwise.

Finishing

Weave in all the loose ends, leaving the ends long until after blocking.

Allow the shawl to soak in lukewarm water until thoroughly saturated. Gently press or spin out the excess water. Block the shawl to the measurements. Allow the shawl to dry completely. Trim all the loose ends.

Monument Valley, also known to the Navajo as Valley of Rocks, appears on the horizon as you travel along the Arizona/Utah border from east to west. Marked with huge sandstone buttes that dominate the landscape, the valley is also filled with undulating rivers of sand shaped by the wind. The area is well-known to fans of many John Ford movies, because he filmed some of his best-known Westerns in this valley, including *Stagecoach*, *Fort Apache*, and *She Wore a Yellow Ribbon*, making the landscape as big a star in his movies as John Wayne himself.

Monument Valley
SWEATER

Finished Size
About 31½ (34¾, 38, 41½, 44¾, 50, 56)" (80 (88.5, 96.5, 105.5, 113.5, 127, 142) cm bust circumference, with 2¼" (5.5 cm) overlap at front bands, and 22¼ (22¾, 23¼, 23¾, 24½, 25¼, 26½)" (56.5 (58, 59, 60.5, 62, 64, 67.5] cm) long.

Project shown measures 34¾" (88.5 cm).

Yarn
Sport weight (#2 Fine).

SHOWN HERE: The Woolen Rabbit Sporty Biffle (100% American wool; 275 yd/3 ½ oz [100 g]): Pumpkin Patch (MC), 4 (4, 5, 5, 6, 7, 8) skeins; Straw (CC), 2 (2, 3, 3, 3, 4, 4) skeins.

Needles
BODY: Size U.S. 4 (3.5 mm) 24" and 40" (60 and 100 cm) long circular (cir).

SLEEVES: Size U.S. 4 (3.5 mm) set of 4 or 5 double-pointed (dpn).

Adjust needle size if necessary to obtain the correct gauge

Notions
Stitch markers (m); stitch holder or waste yarn; tapestry needle; three ¾" (19 mm) buttons, sewing needle; thread.

Gauge
24 sts and 42 rows = 4" (10 cm) in Sand Dune chart, after blocking.

28 sts and 33 rows = 4" (10 cm) in K3, P3 Ribbing, lightly stretched, after blocking.

Notes

The chart is worked back and forth, Read the right-side (odd-numbered) rows from right to left and the wrong-side (even-numbered) rows from left to right.

Circular needles are used to work the body to accommodate the large number of stitches. Work back and forth and do not join.

Because of the stretchy nature of the ribbed side panels, if you wish to wear this piece with a form-fitting shape, choose a size closest to, or a bit smaller than, your actual bust measurement. If you would prefer to wear this with a slightly boxier fit, choose a size a bit larger than your actual bust measurement, or block the ribbing at the side panels so that it lays flat and does not pull in.

STITCH GUIDE

K3, P3 Ribbing *(multiple of 6 sts + 3)*

ROW 1: (RS) *K3, p3; rep from * to last 3 sts, k3.

ROW 2: (WS) *P3, k3; rep from * to last 3 sts, p3.

Rep Rows 1 and 2 for patt.

Back

With shorter cir needle and MC, CO 84 (88, 96, 104, 112, 120, 132) sts using the long-tail cast-on method (see Techniques).

Knit 3 rows.

Beg at right edge of **Sand Dune chart,** work as foll:

ROW 1: (RS) K1, work 2-st rep to last st, k1.

Design Notebook

This woman's hip-length cardigan sweater, with wide-ribbed long sleeves and front bands, also has panels of ribbing at the sides to help shape the sweater. The remainder of the body is worked in a two-colored, textured slip-stitch tweed pattern. The sweater is cast on at the bottom and worked back and forth up to the shoulders in pieces. The ribbed side panels are worked separately and then sewn between the front and back pieces. The shaped-cap sleeves are then cast on and worked from the cuffs up to the shoulders, then sewn into the armholes. The front bands and collar are worked in one piece along the front edges and neckline. Sewn button loops and three buttons are used to close the front.

ROW 2: P1, work 2-st rep to last st, p1.

ROWS 3–8: Work as established.

Rep Rows 1–8 until piece measures 15 (15½, 15½, 15¾, 16, 16½, 17)" (38 [39.5, 39.5, 40, 40.5, 42, 43] cm) from beg, ending with a WS row.

SHAPE ARMHOLES

BO 2 (2, 2, 2, 3, 3, 4) sts at beg of next 2 rows—80 (84, 92, 100, 106, 114, 124) sts rem. Dec 1 st each end of every RS row 1 (1, 1, 1, 2, 2, 3) time(s)—78 (82, 90, 98, 102, 110, 118) sts rem.

Cont even until armholes measure 7¼ (7¼, 7¾, 8, 8½, 8¾, 9½)" (18.5 [18.5, 19.5, 20.5, 21.5, 22, 24] cm), ending with a WS row. Cut CC.

NEXT ROW: (RS) With MC, BO 15 (15, 16, 18, 18, 19, 20) sts, knit until there are 48 (52, 58, 62, 66, 72, 78) sts on right needle tip after BO. BO rem 15 (15, 16, 18, 18, 19, 20) sts. Place rem 48 (54, 58, 62, 66, 72, 78) sts on holder or waste yarn for neck.

Right Front

With shorter cir needle and MC, CO 32 (40, 46, 52, 58, 70, 82) sts using the long-tail cast-on method.

Work same as back until piece measures 15 (15½, 15½, 15¾, 16, 15, 14½)" (38 [39.5, 39.5, 40, 40.5, 38, 37] cm) from beg, ending with a RS row.

SHAPE ARMHOLE AND NECK

Sizes 31½ (34¾, 38, 41½, 44¾)" (80 [88.5, 96.5, 105.5, 113.5] cm) only

BO at beg of WS rows 2 (2, 2, 2, 3) sts once, then 1 st 1 (1, 1, 1, 2) time(s). At the same time, dec 1 st at beg of every RS row 14 (22, 27, 31, 35) times—15 (15, 16, 18, 18) sts rem.

Sizes 50 (56)" (127 [142] cm) only

Dec 1 st at beg of every RS row 46 (55) times. At the same time, when piece measures 16½ (17)" (42 [43] cm) from beg, end with a RS row.

Cont neck shaping, BO at beg of WS rows 3 (4) sts once, then 1 st 2 (3) times—19 (20) sts rem.

All sizes

Cont even until armhole measures 7¼ (7¼, 7¾, 8, 8½, 8¾, 9½)" (18.5 [18.5, 19.5, 20.5, 21.5, 22, 24] cm), ending with a WS row. Cut CC.

With MC, BO all sts kwise.

Left Front

With shorter cir needle and MC, CO 32 (40, 46, 52, 58, 70, 82) sts using the long-tail cast-on method.

Work same as back until piece measures 15 (15½, 15½, 15¾, 16, 15, 14½)" (38 [39.5, 39.5, 40, 40.5, 38, 37] cm) from beg, ending with a WS row.

SHAPE ARMHOLE AND NECK

Sizes 31½ (34¾, 38, 41½, 44¾)" (80 [88.5, 96.5, 105.5, 113.5] cm) only

BO at beg of RS rows 2 (2, 2, 2, 3) sts once, then 1 st 1 (1, 1, 1, 2) time(s). At the same time, dec 1 st at end of every RS row 14 (22, 27, 31, 35) times—15 (15, 16, 18, 18) sts rem.

Sizes 50 (56)" (127 [142] cm) only

Dec 1 st at end of every RS row 46 (55) times. At the same time, when piece measures 16½ (17)" (42 [43] cm) from beg, end with a WS row.

Cont neck shaping, BO at beg of RS rows 3 (4) sts once, then 1 st 2 (3) times—19 (20) sts rem.

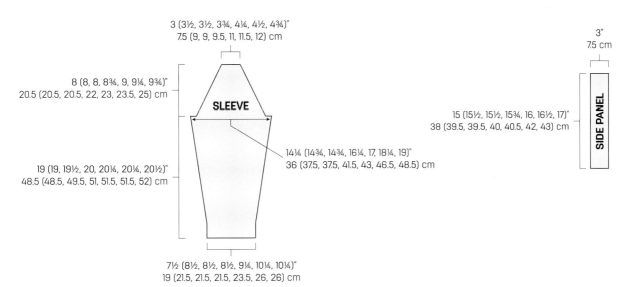

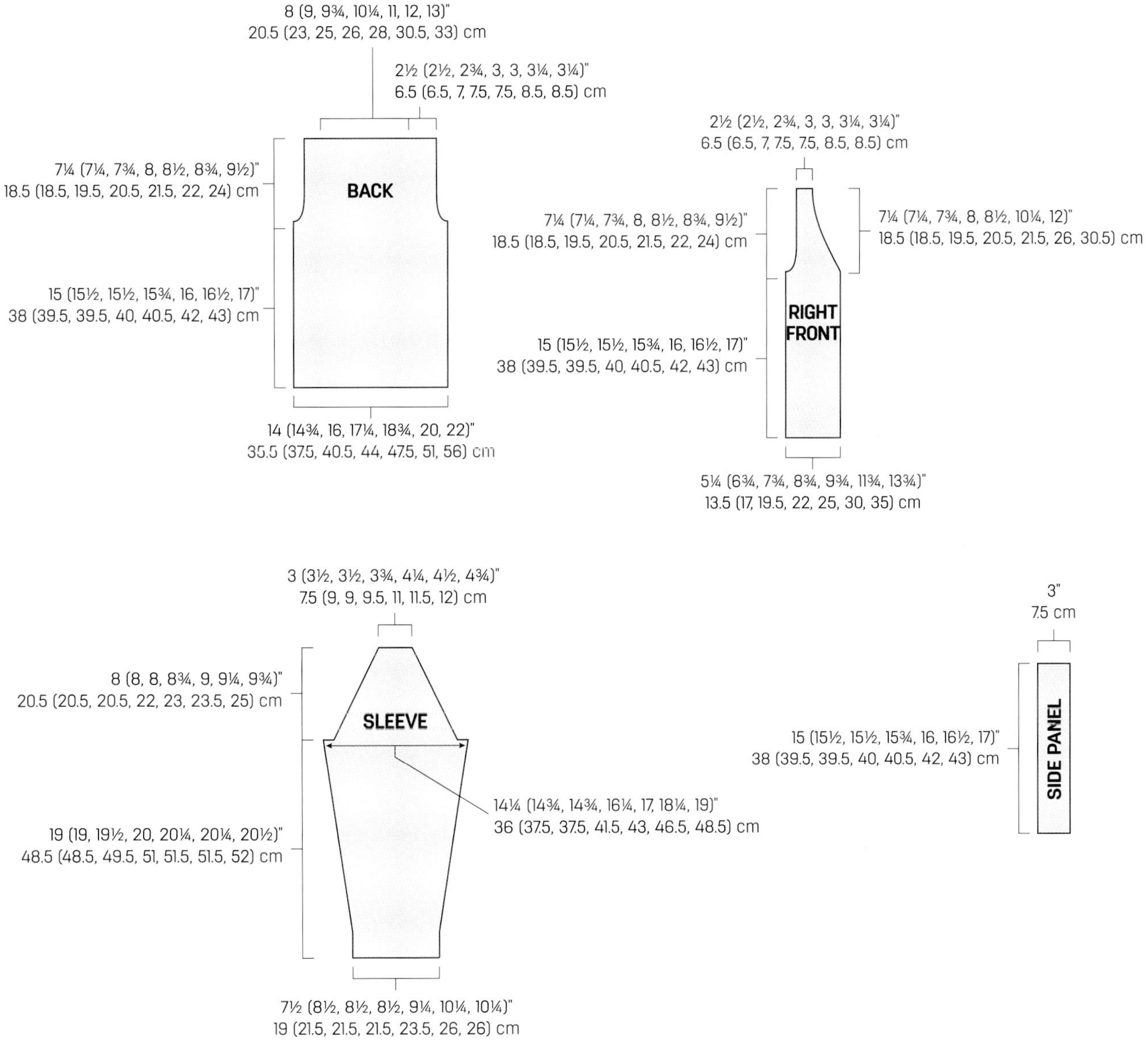

8 (9, 9¾, 10¼, 11, 12, 13)"
20.5 (23, 25, 26, 28, 30.5, 33) cm

2½ (2½, 2¾, 3, 3, 3¼, 3¼)"
6.5 (6.5, 7, 7.5, 7.5, 8.5, 8.5) cm

7¼ (7¼, 7¾, 8, 8½, 8¾, 9½)"
18.5 (18.5, 19.5, 20.5, 21.5, 22, 24) cm

BACK

15 (15½, 15½, 15¾, 16, 16½, 17)"
38 (39.5, 39.5, 40, 40.5, 42, 43) cm

14 (14¾, 16, 17¼, 18¾, 20, 22)"
35.5 (37.5, 40.5, 44, 47.5, 51, 56) cm

2½ (2½, 2¾, 3, 3, 3¼, 3¼)"
6.5 (6.5, 7, 7.5, 7.5, 8.5, 8.5) cm

7¼ (7¼, 7¾, 8, 8½, 8¾, 9½)"
18.5 (18.5, 19.5, 20.5, 21.5, 22, 24) cm

7¼ (7¼, 7¾, 8, 8½, 10¼, 12)"
18.5 (18.5, 19.5, 20.5, 21.5, 26, 30.5) cm

RIGHT FRONT

15 (15½, 15½, 15¾, 16, 16½, 17)"
38 (39.5, 39.5, 40, 40.5, 42, 43) cm

5¼ (6¾, 7¾, 8¾, 9¾, 11¾, 13¾)"
13.5 (17, 19.5, 22, 25, 30, 35) cm

3 (3½, 3½, 3¾, 4¼, 4½, 4¾)"
7.5 (9, 9, 9.5, 11, 11.5, 12) cm

8 (8, 8, 8¾, 9, 9¼, 9¾)"
20.5 (20.5, 20.5, 22, 23, 23.5, 25) cm

SLEEVE

14¼ (14¾, 14¾, 16¼, 17, 18¼, 19)"
36 (37.5, 37.5, 41.5, 43, 46.5, 48.5) cm

19 (19, 19½, 20, 20¼, 20¼, 20½)"
48.5 (48.5, 49.5, 51, 51.5, 51.5, 52) cm

7½ (8½, 8½, 8½, 9¼, 10¼, 10¼)"
19 (21.5, 21.5, 21.5, 23.5, 26, 26) cm

3"
7.5 cm

SIDE PANEL

15 (15½, 15½, 15¾, 16, 16½, 17)"
38 (39.5, 39.5, 40, 40.5, 42, 43) cm

SAND DUNE CHART

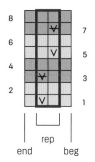

MC

CC

k on RS; p on WS

V sl 1 wyb on RS; sl 1 wyf on WS

V sl 1 wyf on RS; sl 1 wyb on WS

pattern repeat

All sizes

Cont even until armhole measures 7¼ (7¼, 7¾, 8, 8½, 8¾, 9½)" (18.5 [18.5, 19.5, 20.5, 21.5, 22, 24] cm), ending with a WS row. Cut CC.

With MC, BO all sts kwise.

Side Insets

With dpn or short cir needle and MC, CO 21 sts using the long-tail cast-on method.

NEXT ROW: (WS) *P3, k3; rep from * to last 3 sts, p3.

Cont in K3, P3 Ribbing until piece measures 15 (15½, 15½, 15¾, 16, 16½, 17)" (38 [39.5, 39.5, 40, 40.5, 42, 43] cm) from beg, ending with a WS row.

BO all sts loosely in patt.

Sleeves

With dpn and MC, CO 53 (59, 59, 59, 65, 71, 71) sts using the long-tail cast-on method.

NEXT ROW: (WS) P1, *k3, p3; rep from * to last 4 sts, k3, p1.

NEXT ROW: (RS) K1, *p3, k3; rep from * to last 4 sts, p3, k1.

Cont in ribbing as established until piece measures 2½" (6.5 cm) from beg, ending with a WS row.

INC ROW: (RS) K1, m1, work in established ribbing to last st, m1, k1—2 sts inc'd.

Working new sts into ribbing patt, rep Inc row every 4 rows 2 (0, 0, 10, 10, 14, 22) times, then every 6 rows 20 (21, 21, 16, 16, 13, 8) times—99 (103, 103, 113, 119, 127, 133) sts.

Cont even until piece measures 19 (19, 19½, 20, 20¼, 20¼, 20½)" (48.5 [48.5, 49.5, 51, 51.5, 51.5, 52] cm), ending with a WS row.

SHAPE CAP

BO 5 (5, 5, 5, 6, 7, 7) sts at beg of next 2 rows, 3 (3, 3, 4, 4, 5, 5) sts at beg of next 2 rows—83 (87, 87, 95, 99, 103, 109) sts rem.

Dec 1 st each end of every RS row 31 (31, 31, 34, 35, 36, 38) times—21 (25, 25, 27, 29, 31, 33) sts rem.

Work 1 WS row even.

BO all sts in patt.

Finishing

Weave in all the loose ends. Block the pieces to measurements. Sew the side insets to the front and back. Sew the shoulder seams.

NECK/FRONT BAND

With longer cir needle and MC, with RS facing beg at lower right front, pick up and k169 (170, 170, 171, 172, 172, 175) sts along the right front edge to shoulder, knit held 48 (52, 58, 62, 66, 72, 78) back neck sts, pick up and k170 (171, 171, 172, 173, 173, 176) sts along left front edge to bottom edge—387 (393, 399, 405, 411, 417, 429) sts.

NEXT ROW: (WS) *P3, k3; rep from * to last 3 sts, p3.

Cont in established ribbing until band measures 2¼" (5.5 cm).

BO all sts loosely in patt.

Sew underarm seams, sewing about 2½" (6.5 cm) at the cuff on the RS so the seam will not show when the cuff is turned up. Sew the sleeves into the armholes, easing fullness at the center of the cap and lining up the ribbing at the underarm and side insets.

Mark placement for the 3 buttons on left front, placing the buttons at the front band pick-up, placing the bottom button about 9–10" (23–25.5 cm) above bottom edge and spacing the rem 2 buttons about 2" (5 cm) apart.

Note: You may wish to try on the sweater and adjust the button placement as desired. Sew the buttons to the left front.

BUTTON LOOPS

Using tapestry needle threaded with MC, work the 3 sewn button loops opposite the buttons (see Techniques).

The indigenous peoples of the Southwest had many different types of decoration for their pottery, but many utilized a light/dark combination of geometric motifs, similar to those seen in their woven textiles. We are fortunate enough to live near Tsankawi, the lesser known site under the auspices of Bandelier National Monument. By climbing the wooden ladders up to the mesa tops, you can wander along narrow paths worn by centuries of walkers, and if you keep an eye out, you'll be sure to see broken shards of pottery along the paths decorated with these designs.

Pottery Shard JACKET

Finished Size
About 30¼ (32, 34¼, 35¾, 39¾, 43½, 47¼)" (77 [81.5, 87, 91, 101, 110.5, 120] cm) chest circumference, and 21 (21, 21¾, 22, 23, 24, 25)" (53.5 [53.5, 55, 56, 58.5, 61, 63.5] cm) long.

Project shown measures 34¼" (87 cm).

Yarn
Bulky weight (#5 Bulky).

SHOWN HERE: Cascade Yarns Ecological Wool (100% wool; 478 yd/9 oz [250 g]): #8015 Natural (MC), 2 (2, 3, 3, 3, 4, 4) skeins; #8085 Mocha (CC), 1 (1, 1, 1, 1, 2, 2) skein(s).

Needles
BODY: Size U.S. 9 (5.5 mm) 24" (60 cm) or longer circular (cir) and set of 4 or 5 double-pointed (dpn).

SLEEVES: Size U.S. 9 (5.5 mm) set of 4 or 5 double-pointed (dpn).

BANDS: Size U.S. 9 (5.5 mm) 40" (100 cm) or longer circular (cir).

Adjust needle size if necessary to obtain the correct gauge.

Notions
Stitch markers (m); 5 stitch holders; tapestry needle; three 1" (25 mm) buttons; sewing thread; sewing needle.

Gauge
17 sts and 26 rows = 4" (10 cm) in St st and charts, after blocking.

Note: If your gauge over the colorwork sections is different than your St st gauge, you may need to adjust your needle size to maintain a consistent gauge throughout.

Notes

The Band chart is worked back and forth. Read the right-side (odd-numbered) rows from right to left and the wrong-side (even-numbered) rows from left to right. The Cuff chart is worked in the round. Read all rounds from right to left.

Slip the first stitch of each row when knitting the body for a smooth edge to help pick up stitches for the neck and front bands.

A circular needle is used for the body and front band to accommodate the large number of stitches. Work back and forth; do not join. You may find it helpful to use two long circular needles when working the front band.

Design Notebook

This woman's jacket is knit from the bottom up. The body is worked back and forth in stockinette stitch with set-in sleeves. The shawl collar and front bands are worked with geometric shapes in a contrasting color. The front closes with large buttons and knit cord loops. The sleeves are knit from the cuff up, with a stranded knitting pattern of geometric shapes at the cuff.

STITCH GUIDE

Stockinette stitch *(back and forth)*

ROW 1: (RS) Knit.

ROW 2: (WS) Purl.

Rep Rows 1 and 2 for patt.

Stockinette stitch *(worked in the round)*

ALL RNDS: Knit.

Braided Cast-On Method

Holding one strand each of MC and CC together, make a slipknot with both yarns. Place this loop on the right needle (this loop does not count as a cast-on stitch). **HOLD THE STRAND COMING FROM THE BALLS AS FOLLOWS:** the contrasting color yarn around your thumb and the main color yarn around your index finger, holding your palm upward forming a V of yarn as you would for a long-tail cast-on (see Techniques).

Bring needle up through loop on thumb, catch first strand around index finger, and go back down through loop on thumb. Drop loop off thumb and placing thumb back in V configuration, tighten resulting stitch on needle—1 stitch cast on.

Switch the position of both yarns with main color around your thumb and contrasting color around your index finger, moving the color around the index finger under the color around thumb and always moving the yarns in a clockwise direction. Repeat from * to * again to make another stitch.

Switch the position of both yarns again, with the main color around your index finger and the contrasting color around your thumb. Repeat from * to * once more.

Continue casting on stitches in this manner until the required number of stitches have been cast on, making sure to alternate colors with every stitch. Pull the slipknot off the end of the needle.

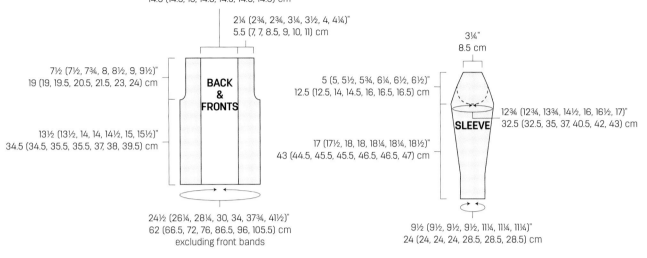

5¾ (5¾, 6, 5¾, 5¾, 5¾, 5¾)"
14.5 (14.5, 15, 14.5, 14.5, 14.5, 14.5) cm

2¼ (2¾, 2¾, 3¼, 3½, 4, 4¼)"
5.5 (7, 7, 8.5, 9, 10, 11) cm

3¼"
8.5 cm

7½ (7½, 7¾, 8, 8½, 9, 9½)"
19 (19, 19.5, 20.5, 21.5, 23, 24) cm

BACK & FRONTS

5 (5, 5½, 5¾, 6¼, 6½, 6½)"
12.5 (12.5, 14, 14.5, 16, 16.5, 16.5) cm

12¾ (12¾, 13¾, 14½, 16, 16½, 17)"
32.5 (32.5, 35, 37, 40.5, 42, 43) cm

SLEEVE

13½ (13½, 14, 14, 14½, 15, 15½)"
34.5 (34.5, 35.5, 35.5, 37, 38, 39.5) cm

17 (17½, 18, 18, 18¼, 18¼, 18½)"
43 (44.5, 45.5, 45.5, 46.5, 46.5, 47) cm

24½ (26¼, 28¼, 30, 34, 37¾, 41½)"
62 (66.5, 72, 76, 86.5, 96, 105.5) cm
excluding front bands

9½ (9½, 9½, 9½, 11¼, 11¼, 11¼)"
24 (24, 24, 24, 28.5, 28.5, 28.5) cm

Body

With cir needle and both colors held together, CO 104 (112, 120, 128, 144, 160, 176) sts using braided cast-on method. Cut CC.

Cont with MC only.

NEXT ROW: (WS) Sl 1, p19 (21, 23, 25, 29, 33, 37), place marker (pm) for left side, p64 (68, 72, 76, 84, 92, 100) sts, pm for right side, k20 (22, 24, 26, 30, 34, 38) sts.

NEXT ROW: (RS) Sl 1, knit to end, slipping m as you come to them.

Cont in St st until piece measures 13½ (13½, 14, 14, 14½, 15, 15½)" (34.5 [34.5, 35.5, 35.5, 37, 38, 39.5] cm) from beg, ending with a RS row.

DIVIDE FRONTS AND BACK
NEXT ROW: (RS) *Work to 4 (4, 5, 5, 6, 6, 7) sts before m, BO next 8 (8, 10, 10, 12, 12, 14) sts for armhole, removing m; rep from * once more, work to end—88 (96, 100, 108, 120, 136, 148) sts rem; 16 (18, 19, 21, 24, 28, 31) sts for each front, and 56 (60, 62, 66, 72, 80, 86) sts for back.

CUFF CHART

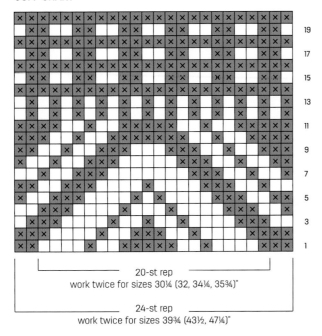

19
17
15
13
11
9
7
5
3
1

20-st rep
work twice for sizes 30¼ (32, 34¼, 35¾)"

24-st rep
work twice for sizes 39¾ (43½, 47¼)"

BAND CHART

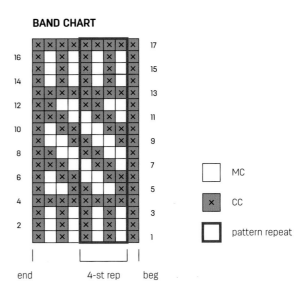

17
16
15
14
13
12
11
10
9
8
7
6
5
4
3
2
1

end   4-st rep   beg

□ MC
☒ CC
□ pattern repeat

Right Front

SHAPE ARMHOLE
Work 1 RS row even.

NEXT ROW: (WS) BO 3, purl to end—13 (15, 16, 18, 21, 25, 28) sts rem.

Dec 1 st at end of every RS row 3 (3, 4, 4, 6, 8, 10) times—10 (12, 12, 14, 15, 17, 18) sts rem.

Cont even until armhole measures 7½ (7½, 7¾, 8, 8½, 9, 9½)" (19 [19, 19.5, 20.5, 21.5, 23, 24] cm), ending with a WS row. Place rem sts on holder.

Back

SHAPE ARMHOLES
Rejoin MC to beg with a RS row. BO 3 sts at beg of next 2 rows—50 (54, 56, 60, 66, 74, 80) sts rem.

Dec 1 st each end every RS row 3 (3, 3, 4, 6, 8, 10) times—44 (48, 50, 52, 54, 58, 60) sts rem.

Cont even until armholes measure 7½ (7½, 7¾, 8, 8½, 9, 9½)" (19 [19, 19.5, 20.5, 21.5, 23, 24] cm), ending with a WS row. Cut yarn. Place first 10 (12, 12, 14, 15, 17, 18) sts on holder for shoulder, center 24 (24, 26, 24, 24, 24, 24) sts on holder for neck, then rem 10 (12, 12, 14, 15, 17, 18) sts on holder for shoulder.

Left Front

SHAPE ARMHOLE
Rejoin MC to beg with a WS row.

Purl 1 WS row even.

NEXT ROW: (RS) BO 3 sts, knit to end—13 (15, 16, 18, 21, 25, 28) sts rem.

Dec 1 st at end of every RS row 3 (3, 4, 4, 6, 8, 10) times—10 (12, 12, 14, 15, 17, 18) sts rem.

Cont evenly until piece measures 7½ (7½, 7¾, 8, 8½, 9, 9½)" (19 (19, 19.5, 20.5, 21.5, 23, 24] cm), ending with a WS row. Place rem sts on holder.

Sleeves

With dpn and both colors held together, CO 40 (40, 40, 40, 48, 48, 48) sts using the braided cast-on method. Pm and join for working in rnds, being careful not to twist sts. Leave both yarns attached.

Knit 1 rnd with CC.

NEXT RND: Beg Rnd 1 of *Cuff chart* for your size, work 20- (20-, 20-, 20-, 24-, 24-, 24-) st rep of Row 1 twice.

Work Rnds 2–20 as established. Cut CC.

Cont with MC only, knit 1 rnd.

INC RND: K1, m1l, knit to last st, m1r, k1—2 sts inc'd.

Rep Inc rnd every 12 (12, 10, 8, 8, 8, 6) rnds 6 (6, 8, 10, 4, 8, 3) times, then every 0 (0, 0, 0, 10, 10, 8) rnds 0 (0, 0, 0, 5, 2, 8) times—54 (54, 58, 62, 68, 70, 72) sts.

Cont even until piece measures 17 (17½, 18, 18, 18¼, 18¼, 18½)" (43 [44.5, 45.5, 45.5, 46.5, 46.5, 47] cm), ending last rnd 4 (4, 5, 5, 6, 6, 7) sts before end of rnd.

SHAPE CAP

BO 8 (8, 10, 10, 12, 12, 14) sts, knit to end—46 (46, 48, 52, 56, 58, 58) sts rem

BO 3 sts at beg of next 2 rows. Dec 1 st each end of every RS row 11 (11, 12, 15, 17, 18, 18) times, then every 4 rows 2 (2, 2, 1, 1, 1, 1) time(s)—14 sts rem.

BO rem sts.

Finishing

Join the shoulders using the three-needle bind-off (see Techniques).

NECK AND FRONT BAND

With longer cir needle(s) and CC, with RS facing, beg at lower right edge, pick up and k93 (93, 96, 97, 101, 105, 105) sts along right front edge to shoulder, k24 (24, 26, 24, 24, 24, 24) held sts of back neck, then pick up and k92 (92, 95, 96, 100, 104, 104) sts along left front edge—209 (209, 217, 217, 225, 233, 233) sts.

Purl 1 WS row.

NEXT ROW: (RS) Beg with Row 1 at right edge of *Band chart*, knit first st, work 4-st rep to last 4 sts, work last 4 sts at left edge of chart.

NEXT ROW: (WS) Beg at left edge of Row 2 of chart, work first 4 sts, work 4-st rep to last st, work last st at right edge of chart.

Work Rows 3–17 of chart as established. Cut MC.

TURNING ROW: (WS) With CC, knit.

Work 16 rows in St st.

Cut yarn, leaving about 65" (165 cm) long tail. Thread tail into a tapestry needle. Fold the band to the inside along the turning row and whipstitch sts to the band pick-up row. Sew the band together along the lower edges.

BUTTON LOOPS (MAKE 3)

With 2 dpn and both colors held together, CO 12 sts using the braided cast-on method, leaving 6" (15 cm) long tails. Cut MC.

With CC only, BO all sts kwise. Cut yarn, leaving 6" (15 cm) long tail.

Mark placement for the 3 buttons on the left band, placing the middle button 9" to 10" (23–25.5 cm) from the bottom edge, or at your natural waistline, and 1" (2.5 cm) from the fold edge, and space rem 2 buttons 2½" (6.5 cm) above and below the center button.

Thread CC tail into tapestry needle, sew loops to the fold edge of the right band opposite the button m and about ½" (1.3 cm) between loop ends.

Weave in all the loose ends. Allow the pieces to soak in lukewarm water until thoroughly saturated. Gently press or spin out the excess water. Block all the pieces to measurements, pinning hems and bands to lay flat. Allow the pieces to dry completely.

Sew in sleeves. Sew buttons to left band opposite button loops.

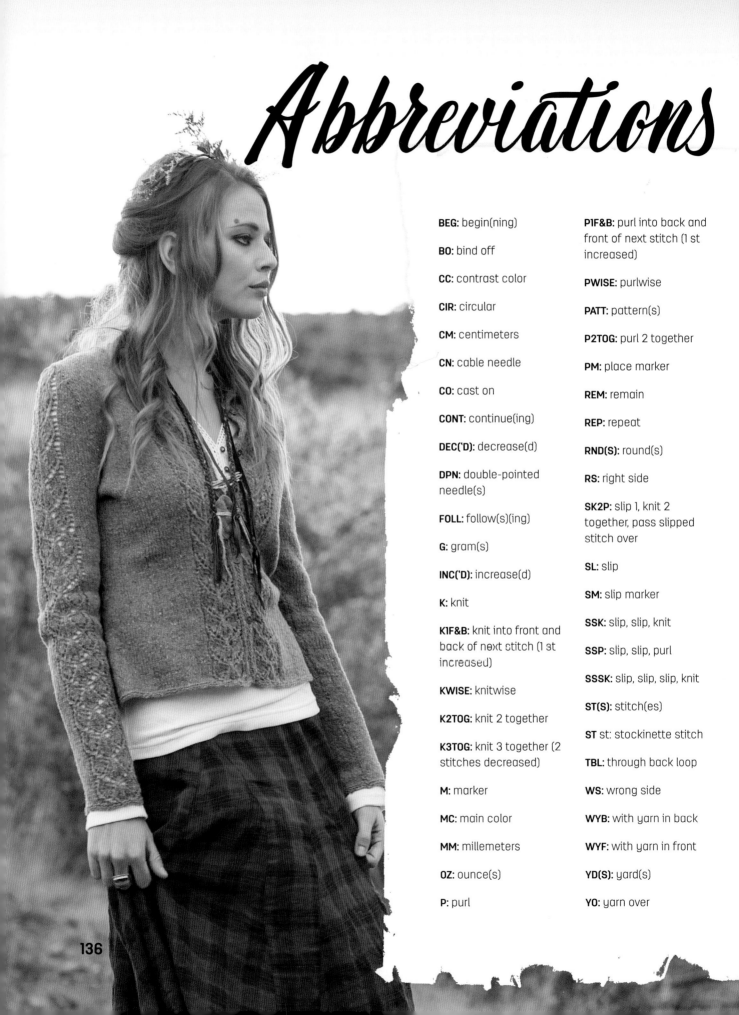

Abbreviations

BEG: begin(ning)

BO: bind off

CC: contrast color

CIR: circular

CM: centimeters

CN: cable needle

CO: cast on

CONT: continue(ing)

DEC('D): decrease(d)

DPN: double-pointed needle(s)

FOLL: follow(s)(ing)

G: gram(s)

INC('D): increase(d)

K: knit

K1F&B: knit into front and back of next stitch (1 st increased)

KWISE: knitwise

K2TOG: knit 2 together

K3TOG: knit 3 together (2 stitches decreased)

M: marker

MC: main color

MM: millemeters

OZ: ounce(s)

P: purl

P1F&B: purl into back and front of next stitch (1 st increased)

PWISE: purlwise

PATT: pattern(s)

P2TOG: purl 2 together

PM: place marker

REM: remain

REP: repeat

RND(S): round(s)

RS: right side

SK2P: slip 1, knit 2 together, pass slipped stitch over

SL: slip

SM: slip marker

SSK: slip, slip, knit

SSP: slip, slip, purl

SSSK: slip, slip, slip, knit

ST(S): stitch(es)

ST st: stockinette stitch

TBL: through back loop

WS: wrong side

WYB: with yarn in back

WYF: with yarn in front

YD(S): yard(s)

YO: yarn over

Techniques

CAST-ONS

Backward-Loop Cast-On

*Loop working yarn and place it on needle backward so that it doesn't unwind. Repeat from *.

Cable Cast-On

If there are no stitches on the needles, make a slip-knot of working yarn and place it on the needle, then use the knitted method to cast on one more stitch— two stitches on needle. Hold needle with working yarn in your left hand. *Insert right needle between the first two stitches on left needle *(Figure 1)*, wrap yarn around needle as if to knit, draw yarn through *(Figure 2),* and place new loop on left needle *(Figure 3)* to form a new stitch. Repeat from * for the desired number of stitches, always working between the first two stitches on the left needle.

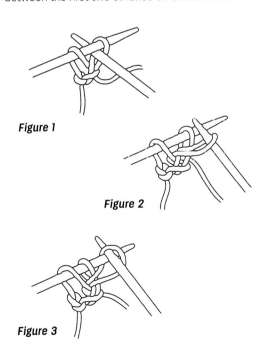

Figure 1

Figure 2

Figure 3

Long-Tail Cast-On

Leaving a long tail (about ½" [1.3 cm] for each stitch to be cast on), make a slipknot and place on right needle. Place thumb and index finger of your left hand between the yarn ends so that working yarn is around your index finger and tail end is around your thumb and secure the yarn ends with your other fingers.

Hold your palm upward, making a V of yarn *(Figure 1)*. *Bring needle up through loop on thumb *(Figure 2)*, catch first strand around index finger, and go back down through loop on thumb *(Figure 3)*. Drop loop off thumb and, placing thumb back in V configuration, tighten resulting stitch on needle *(Figure 4)*. Repeat from * for the desired number of stitches.

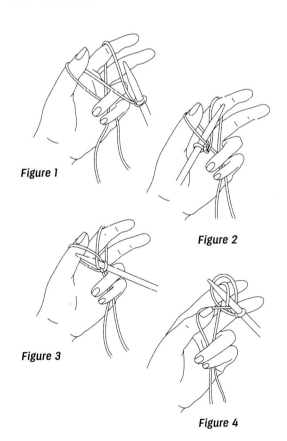

Figure 1

Figure 2

Figure 3

Figure 4

Provisional Cast-On

With waste yarn and crochet hook, make a loose crochet chain about four stitches more than you need to
cast on. With knitting needle, working yarn, and beginning two stitches from end of chain, pick up and knit
one stitch through the back loop of each crochet chain
(Figure 1) for desired number of stitches. When you're
ready to work in the opposite direction, pull out the
crochet chain to expose live stitches *(Figure 2).*

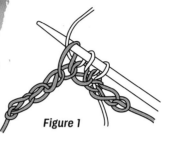

Figure 1

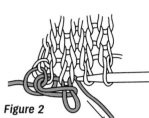

Figure 2

BIND-OFFS

Three-Needle Bind-Off

Place the stitches to be joined onto two separate
needles and hold the needles parallel so that the right
sides of knitting face together. Insert a third needle into
the first stitch on each of two needles *(Figure 1)* and
knit them together as one stitch *(Figure 2),* *knit the
next stitch on each needle the same way, then use
the left needle tip to lift the first stitch over the second
and off the needle *(Figure 3).* Repeat from * until no
stitches remain on first two needles. Cut yarn and pull
tail through last stitch to secure.

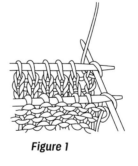

Figure 1

Figure 2

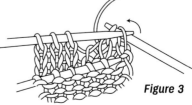

Figure 3

Sewn Bind-Off

This method, worked using a tapestry needle, forms an elastic edge that has a ropy appearance much like a cast-on edge. It is ideal for finishing off garter stitch.

Cut the yarn, leaving a tail about three times the width of the knitting to be bound off, and thread the tail onto a tapestry needle.

Working from right to left, *insert the tapestry needle purlwise (from right to left) through the first two stitches on the left needle tip *(Figure 1)* and pull the yarn through. Bring tapestry needle through the first stitch again, but this time knitwise (from left to right; *Figure 2*), pull the yarn through, then slip this stitch off the knitting needle.

Repeat from * for the desired number of stitches.

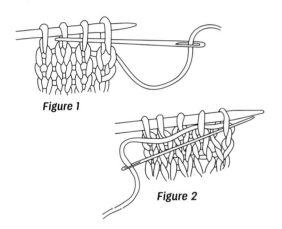

Figure 1

Figure 2

INCREASES
Raised (M1) Increases

With left needle tip, lift strand between needles from front to back *(Figure 1)*. Knit lifted loop through the back *(Figure 2)*.

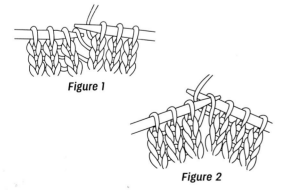

Figure 1

Figure 2

Right Slant (M1R)

With left needle tip, lift strand between needles from back to front *(Figure 1)*. Knit lifted loop through the front *(Figure 2)*.

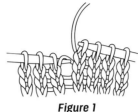

Figure 1   *Figure 2*

GRAFTING
Kitchener Stitch
(St st Grafting)

STEP 1: Bring threaded needle through front stitch as if to purl and leave stitch on needle *(Figure 1)*.

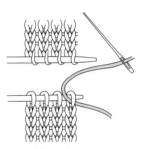

Figure 1

STEP 2: Bring threaded needle through back stitch as if to knit and leave stitch on needle *(Figure 2)*.

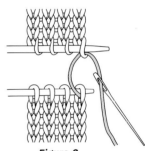

Figure 2

STEP 3: Bring threaded needle through first front stitch as if to knit and slip this stitch off needle. Bring threaded needle through next front stitch as if to purl and leave stitch on needle *(Figure 3)*.

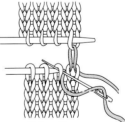

Figure 3

STEP 4: Bring threaded needle through first back stitch as if to purl (as illustrated), slip this stitch off, bring needle through next back stitch as if to knit, leave this stitch on needle *(Figure 4)*.

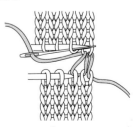

Figure 4

Repeat Steps 3 and 4 until no stitches remain on needles.

Placing Beads Using a Crochet Hook

Work to the stitch designated for bead placement, work the stitch as specified in the instruction, slip a bead onto the shaft of a crochet hook, remove the knitted stitch from the knitting needle, and lift the stitch just worked with the hook. **(Figure 1).** Slide the bead onto the stitch just worked, return that stitch to the left needle, adjust the tension, then slip that stitch onto the right knitting needle **(Figure 2).**

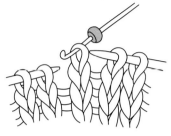

Sources for Yarn

THE ALPACA YARN COMPANY
144 Roosevelt Ave., Bay #1
York, PA 17401
thealpacayarnco.com

BAAH!
baahyarn.com

BERROCO
1 Tupperware Dr., Ste. 4
North Smithfield, RI 02896
(401) 769-1212
berroco.com

BROOKLYN TWEED
Brooklyntweed.net

CASCADE
PO Box 58168 1224
Andover Park E.
Tukwila, WA 98188
cascadeyarns.com

CLASSIC ELITE YARNS
16 Esquire Rd. Unit 2
North Billerica, MA 01862
classiceliteyarns.com

DREAM IN COLOR
dreamincoloryarn.com

ELEMENTAL AFFECTS
17555 Bubbling Wells Rd.
Desert Hot Springs, CA 92241
(888) 699-2919

GREEN MOUNTAIN SPINNERY
Box 568
Putney, VT 05346
(802) 387-4528
cpinncry.com

HARRISVILLE DESIGNS
4 Mill Alley
Harrisville, NH 03450
(603) 827-3996

JAMIESON & SMITH
shetlandwoolbrokers.co.uk

THE FIBRE COMPANY
Distributed by Kelbourne
Woolens
2000 Manor Rd.
Conshohocken, PA 19428
kelbournewoolens.com

ROWAN
Green Lane Mill
Holmfirth, West Yorkshire
England HD9 2DX
44 (0)1484 681881
knitrowan.com
USA:
Westminster Fibers
165 Ledge St.
Nashua, NH 03060
(800) 445-9276
westminsterfibers.com

SNOWSHOE FARM ALPACAS
(802) 592-3153
vermontalpacayarn.com

SWEET GEORGIA
110-408 East Kent Ave. S.
Vancouver, BC
Canada V5X 2X7
sweetgeorgiayarns.com

WEBS/VALLEY YARNS
yarn.com/webs-knitting-crochet-yarns-valley-yarns

THE WOOLEN RABBIT
PO Box 1415
131 Pleasant St.
Conway, NH 03818
thewoolenrabbit.com

WOOLY WONKA FIBER
woolywonkafiber.com

Acknowledgments

TO ANDI, JULIE, SUSAN AND TOBY: Thank you for helping me get all the sample knits finished on time. **TO AUDREY, DEB, HEIKE, MAYTE, SIMONE:** Thank you all for test knitting the projects for me. **TO MAUREEN AND LORI:** Thank you for casting a critical eye over the numbers and text for me. **TO DAVE:** For understanding when I needed to "just finish this sweater/shawl/sock before dinner" on many nights. You are my biggest fan and greatest supporter.

Index

ACQUISITIONS EDITOR
Kerry Bogert

EDITOR
Erica Smith

TECHNICAL EDITOR
Therese Chynoweth

PHOTOGRAPHER
Joe Hancock

HAIR AND MAKEUP
Kathy MacKay

STYLING
Tina Gill

ART DIRECTOR
Charlene Tiedemann

COVER AND INTERIOR DESIGN
Charlene Tiedemann

 Interweave
A division of F+W Media, Inc.
4868 Innovation Dr.
Fort Collins, CO 80525
interweave.com

Manufactured in China by
RR Donnelley Shenzhen

ISBN 978-1-62033-949-7 (pbk.)
ISBN 978-1-62033-950-3 (PDF)

10 9 8 7 6 5 4 3 2 1

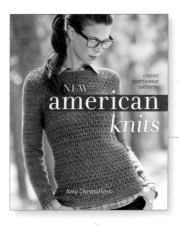